TOP DOWN

TOP DOWN

Why Hierarchies Are
Here to Stay and How to
Manage Them More Effectively

Harold J. Leavitt

HARVARD BUSINESS SCHOOL PRESS
BOSTON, MASSACHUSETTS

Library of Congress Cataloging-in-Publication Data
Leavitt, Harold J.
    Top down : why hierarchies are here to stay and how to manage them more
    effectively / Harold J. Leavitt.
        p. cm.
    ISBN 1-59139-498-8
    1. Management. 2. Hierarchies. 3. Executive ability. 4. Employee
empowerment. 5. Organizational effectiveness. I. Title.
    HD31.L354 2005
    658.4—dc22

                                                            2004010145

For Jean
Dear companion, uncompromising critic.
We write for one another

CONTENTS

PREFACE

People write books for all sorts of strange reasons. At first, this one was motivated mostly by my annoyance at those of my colleagues who study and write about organizations. It seemed to me that too many of us were becoming victims of our own propaganda. We were beginning to believe what we wanted to believe, that those cruel, inhumane, inefficient, authoritarian hierarchical organizations were really passé. We were telling the world that organizations were about to abandon, or had already abandoned, the old, multi-tiered, top-down designs in favor of new networks, communities, federalized systems, internal market structures, and other, more egalitarian forms.

It's not that the critics are wrong in asserting that hierarchies tend to be difficult places for human beings to work. That's indisputable. While doing a pretty good job of facilitating enormously complex tasks, hierarchies invariably spew out all sorts of noxious by-products. They generate distrust, fear, conflict, servility, greed, and a host of other debilitating fumes. And these poisons cause them to leak much of their projected efficiency.

Nevertheless, they're here to stay.

I agree that organizations are making many positive changes—in response to cascading technology and to shifts in social attitudes and beliefs—but are these changes really supplanting top-down, hierarchical architectures? Not in the organizational world that I know. Softening up hierarchies, yes. Building in more horizontal communication channels, yes. Putting more emphasis on collaborative teams and small groups, yes. Forming alliances and interorganizational connections, yes. Organizations are certainly changing in these and other important ways. But replacing hierarchies? No!

Multilevel, pyramid-shaped structures remain solidly in place. Many are being remodeled, perhaps, but their basic hierarchical architecture has not gone away. Aren't large organizations still made up of multiple ranks, bosses piled on bosses, and carefully orchestrated differences in power, control, rewards, and all the rest? Aren't such tiered differences the defining characteristics of most large human organizations?

This book is not a defense of hierarchies. I have observed and personally encountered too many of their destructive failings. So I have been something of a proselytizer for ways to make hierarchies better for people—from long-ago experiments with communication networks, to early work in organizational psychology, to more recent writings on hot groups.[1] I certainly applaud current horizontalizing as well as many other humanizing improvements such as flattening, team building, and networking.

Nevertheless, reality is reality. This is not the first time some of us have celebrated the impending end of hierarchies. It has happened repeatedly over the past seven or eight decades. But the end has never come. Much as one might wish otherwise, the organizational innovations of recent years can hardly be construed as replacements for hierarchies. Words such as *power, control,* and *authority* still pervade the organizational atmosphere. Young managers still struggle to climb hierarchical ladders, and they continue to complain about their unfair performance appraisals. Hierarchies, it seems obvious, still dominate the stage, even in enlightened modern organizations. And, I might add, people who actually work in these organizations appear to know that better than some sages.

Many of us wish hierarchies would go away because their authoritarian character doesn't jibe with our egalitarian societal values. That's doubtless why today's organizational authoritarianism is often cloaked in a veil of humanism. But behind the veil, top-down power and control are still there. Indeed, the hierarchical form in large modern organizations may arguably be waxing not waning, helped more than hindered by galloping advances in technology.

If today's large organizations are indeed basically hierarchical, two questions immediately arise. The first is why? If the form is so ill suited to contemporary social values and to our new knowledge-based, informational world, then why, despite wishful assertions to the contrary, is it still with us? Part I of this book looks for answers to that question.

A second query follows from the first: So what? Everyone who works inside a big organization knows it's hierarchical, so why make a big deal of it? There is, I think, a good reason to make at least a small deal of it: An important disconnect is taking place; a disconnect between those end-of-hierarchy views held by many management experts and the realities of everyday working life inside ongoing hierarchical organizations. This seems especially true for the large, ill-defined cadre of workers called "middle management."

Middle managers are being bombarded with mixed signals. Their companies look to them to implement multiple, sometimes mutually exclusive changes—the big changes that their organizations want to integrate into their corporate cultures. Middle managers must manage more participatively, more collaboratively, and more creatively, but more systematically, more tightly, and more rapidly, too.

I have taught and worked with many middle managers in many parts of the world over many years. They are, with rare exceptions, dedicated people, trying to do good work under increasingly perplexing and inchoate conditions. So although this is something of a contrarian book, questioning current assertions about the impending demise of hierarchies, it also tries to be a helpful book, reminding middle managers that they breathe hierarchical air and swim in authoritarian seas. Importantly, this book goes on to offer what I hope will be useful advice about the skills, personal qualities, and understandings that middle (and other) managers may need if they are to find success and meaning as they labor in today's authoritarian surroundings.

A NOTE OF THANKS

Here are only a few of those who have helped and inspired: my colleagues past and present at Stanford and elsewhere; the executive and middle managers from whom I have learned so much; sons John and David for sharp observations and offbeat ideas; Robert and Bonnie Fisher for their good questioning and patient listening; Connie Martinson of *Connie Martinson Talks Books* for her deep savvy; Diane Coutu for forcing me to edit and reedit the *HBR* article that spawned this book; our ever-ready, no-nonsense agent, Denise Marcil; my gently persistent editor, Jacqueline Murphy; and three anonymous reviewers, whose criticisms and suggestions were of immense help.

My special thanks to Heather Fraschetti, our bright, utterly dependable, mostly unflappable aide-de-camp. She maintained order amidst chaos, responded to computer-related eruptions with calm and competence, and helped in a thousand other ways.

And then there's Jean—it simply couldn't have happened without her.

Alive, Well, and Everywhere*

*Men are forever creating organizations for their
own convenience and forever finding themselves the
victims of their home-made monsters.*

—Aldous Huxley

Hierarchy, that oldest and most controlling attribute of large human organizations, shouldn't just go on and on, but it does. It shouldn't, because those multilevel, pyramid-shaped structures are authoritarian. They breed infantilizing dependency that generates distrust, conflict, toadying, territoriality, backstabbing, distorted communication, and most of the other ailments that plague every large organization. Nevertheless, almost every large human organization, past and present, was and is hierarchical.

Hierarchies are, as they have been for centuries, "normal" and prevalent everywhere. The hierarchical pyramid is probably the single

---

*Portions of this and other chapters use segments from the author's essay "Why Hierarchies Thrive" in the March 2003 issue of the *Harvard Business Review*.

element we are most likely to envision when we hear the word *organization*. Hierarchies pervade democracies, theocracies, oligarchies, monarchies, and autocracies. They're the standard in every type of institution, from judicial systems to universities to governments to businesses to trade unions. They're commonplace, perhaps especially so in societies that profess to abhor inequality, such as the old Soviet Union and China. They have existed in all sorts of nonhuman systems since the woolly mammoth roamed our world. Beyond this earthly realm, they are even rife in heaven, we're told: "There is . . . a necessary gradation among hierarchs . . . even among the angels, i.e., in the heavenly hierarchy. The hierarchy, therefore, connotes the totality of powers established in the Church for the guiding of man to his eternal salvation, but divided into various orders or grades, in which the inferior are subject to and yield obedience to the higher ones."[1]

For readers untutored in such celestial matters, here is the rank order of precedence in that heavenly hierarchy:

1. Seraphim

2. Cherubim

3. Dominations

4. Thrones

5. Principalities

6. Potentates

7. Virtues

8. Archangels

9. Just plain Angels[2]

This nearly universal hierarchical architecture has a great many advantages, but, in its human form, it certainly isn't angelic. Large human hierarchies push people around, often unfairly and arbitrarily. They frustrate the simple application of human intelligence. They are forever throwing bureaucratic obstacles into the paths of good work. Their vertical designs violate the norms and values of horizontal, egalitarian societies. They're slow and ponderous—or at least they're caricatured that way—and their tendency to distort communication is notorious.

Of course, there are hierarchies, and there are hierarchies. There is great variation among the human ones and even more among their nonhuman forms—ranging from hierarchical computer programs to biological and other hierarchies in nature. These nonhuman members of the hierarchical genus are not the central focus of this book because they do not generate psychological issues such as authority and dependency.

This book is mostly about large *human* hierarchies and the people who work in them. Its focus is on the tensions that build between these inevitable hierarchies and the needs and values of human beings, especially as these tensions play out in the lives and work of managers.

ARE HIERARCHIES REALLY ON THEIR WAY OUT?

Hierarchies in organizations are patently obvious, and they have been that way for a long time. So why bother to prove the world is still round? It's because many very sensible people don't quite see it that way. Some people—those who are especially concerned with human welfare—might agree that hierarchies are commonplace, but feel they're so bad for people that we should get rid of them. Other observers—those who are more concerned about effectiveness of organizations—believe that hierarchical architecture is just out of date, as old-fashioned as spats, inefficient as well as inhumane. Must we really, in today's world of knowledge and information, still deal with hierarchies' archaic appendages, things like ranks and statuses and charts showing who reports to whom?

Some of the detractors of hierarchies go further than that. Even a cursory scan of current professional books and papers on organizational design, leadership, and general management shows that, if they mention hierarchies at all, they tend to present them as relics of the past. Again and again thoughtful scholars assure us that large hierarchies are either extinct or about to expire. Thus Warren Bennis quotes as wise an observer as Peter Drucker forecasting (in 1989) an *orchestral* successor to the archaic hierarchy:

> *We are witnessing what may be the death of the large organiza-*
> *tion . . . The flagships of the last forty years, institutions like Gen-*
> *eral Motors, ITT, and DuPont, have basically outlived their useful-*
> *ness . . . I think they're past their peaks. There's very little flexibility*
> *there, very little creativity . . . You know, elephants don't do well*
> *in confined spaces . . . The model organization of tomorrow is the*
> *symphony orchestra. Have you ever witnessed the performance of a*
> *late Mahler symphony with 1,000 people on stage? Now if you tried*
> *our normal organization, you'd have the chief executive conductor,*
> *six chief operating conductors, and about twenty-two department*
> *conductors. Instead of which you'll have only one conductor.*[3]

That was Drucker in 1989. Fifteen years later, in 2004, GM, ITT, and DuPont continue to chug along, but it is certainly true that many other big companies—Polaroid, Kmart, Montgomery Ward—have indeed succumbed or come close to it. So are we truly in the midst of a shift away from the multilevel hierarchy toward more orchestral forms? And if we are heading in that direction, do we really want to go there? Is the ideal future organization one that is under the total control of a single, nearly omnipotent leader, a leader who demands and receives instantaneous obedience from the masses he or she commands? And wouldn't even such a structure still be hierarchical?

A decade after Drucker's observation, Gifford Pinchot, in a 1998 article titled "An Alternative to Hierarchy," argues that "hierarchical organizations based on dominance and submission" are about to be replaced, not by orchestras, but by *community*.[4] And more recently still, in 2002, Cloke and Goldsmith, in their good book *The End of Management and the Rise of Organizational Democracy*, also go after hierarchies. They see "an increasing urgency in the demand for a new organizational order and the frustration that many employees and leaders at all levels feel with pointless layers of hierarchy, egotistical leadership, autocratic decision making, bureaucratic bungling,

wasted time and effort, managerial incompetence, petty microman-
agement, and employee resistance to developing more mature, responsible, collaborative work relationships."[5]

Moreover, while browsing through a 1995 book that celebrated
the writings of the extraordinary organizational activist Mary Parker
Follett, I learned that, back in the 1920s, she, too, forecast the im-
pending demise of hierarchical bureaucracies. But then, Harvard
Business School Professor Nitin Nohria, in his commentary on a
Follett essay, wrote something I found both unusual and admirable:

> In 1988 . . . Bob [Eccles] and I were both convinced . . . that the
> hierarchical bureaucracy—the dominant organizational model
> since the turn of [the twentieth] century—was rapidly becoming
> obsolete. Two years and hundreds of interviews later, we wrote up
> what we had learned. . . . But like everyone else writing about the
> new organization, we could not say that we had actually studied
> even one organization that exhibited all the characteristics we
> had identified [My emphasis].[6]

The reality seems to be that a great many scholars, educators,
consultants, and executives simply don't like what large hierarchies
do to people and to productivity. So, optimists that we are, we keep
dancing on their unoccupied graves, decade after decade, generation
after generation. Large hierarchies, we keep averring, are in extremis,
kaput, moribund. Their hidden burial ground lies just beyond the
horizon, where it has lain for at least eighty years.

What does all this mean? What does it mean for the field of organizational studies, and, more important, what does it mean for the
middle manager, a major target of the writings and educational programs those pronouncements keep spawning? Why have realistic Follett in the 1920s, observant scholar Nohria in the 1990s, and a great
many sensible others in between and since, all been wrong? Perhaps
we have all fallen into a familiar psychological trap, one we humans
frequently fall prey to. Given the choice between our faiths and
our observations, we have a propensity to modify our observations
toward consistency with our faiths, and not the other way round.

Would that the end of all that hierarchical detritus were really in sight. It isn't. And those aspiring to the managerial life had better be aware that it isn't. Would that hierarchies were right now being supplanted by other designs—by horizontal or circular structures more appropriate to our high-tech times, more befitting our free society, and more liberating for organizations' members. They aren't. Old, steeply vertical hierarchies are indeed changing—somewhat. Some are flattening. Others are giving their people more autonomy, but many of those are also keeping a closer, Big Brotherly electronic eye on them. Many are opening multiple horizontal and diagonal linkages. And many are now treating *groups,* long in disfavor in traditional, individual-based hierarchies, somewhat more tolerantly. These changes are generally positive, but they haven't eliminated hierarchy.

Many previously steep hierarchical structures have flattened, loosened, or otherwise modified themselves. Such upgrades to indoor plumbing surely improve things. But hierarchies remain the predominant structural forms of large organizations, as real as the air we breathe and often just as impure.

It's not that some organizations haven't experimented with real alternative designs. Back in the wilder days of the late 1960s, for example, I watched a graduate professional school in a major university try to do just that. It reorganized itself from a conventional form—dean, faculty, administrative staff, and so on—into a "true democracy." Staff, professors, alumni, students, and maintenance crew all became equal partners—one person, one vote—on all significant decisions. At crowded, noisy meetings, the entire community voted on selection of new faculty and incoming students and decided on promotions, salaries, and other school policies and practices. It was a brief, chaotic, and wholly unsuccessful experiment.

When there was still a unified socialist Yugoslavia, the Yugoslavs also tried to turn the hierarchy on its head. They made a small bow to capitalism by introducing a "self-management" system. Workers elected their company's board from their own ranks. The board then recruited a managing director, a CEO. The new CEO's job was to direct the workers, at the pleasure (as in Western capitalist countries) of the board, which really meant at the pleasure of the workers the CEO was directing. The system didn't work very well. The turn-over rate among managing directors became rather high. Nor did the new scheme supplant the hierarchy. The bottom of the hierarchy just threw a lasso around the top—and pulled.

Present-day organizations play down their hierarchical nature, as though it embarrasses them. Our organizational language is full of authority-disguising euphemisms. When, for example, a senior ex-ecutive says of a junior colleague, "Joe isn't a team player," does it mean that Joe isn't an effective team member? Or does it really mean—in organization-speak—that Joe doesn't do as he's told? At one company I knew, people would say, "Mary was stimulated yes-terday." It took me a while to discover that *stimulated* meant *fired.* Mary had been stimulated to depart the premises. And some Euro-peans feel that our American propensity for almost instant use of first names, regardless of hierarchical rank, is only another effort to sugarcoat reality, to obfuscate the authoritarian hierarchy's inconsis-tency with our culture's trumpeted egalitarian values.

Plus Ça Change . . .

Authority and the power that attaches to it are still distributed unequally, with some members having much more of it than oth-ers, and certain people thereby determining other people's orga-nizational fates. These planned differences in status, power, and resources were realities a hundred years ago, they're realities to-day, and they dominate all other human concerns in large human organizations.

It is true that a few organizations may not be structured as hier-archies. Some small start-ups, for example, operate in quite open, egalitarian ways. But wait until those little guys grow older and larger. Then hierarchy will come creeping in, and bundled with it will come layers of regulations, control systems, and all the rest. If we search very hard, we may perhaps find a few other *almost* nonhierarchical institutions, perhaps the Quakers or some very early universities— as Oxford and Cambridge once were—or some relatively isolated tribal communities. But those are rare and probably not entirely hierarchy-free.

"All Organizations Are Prisons"

Long ago, in the days of Rockefeller and Ford, our attitudes toward organizational hierarchies were different. We used to extol their blatantly authoritarian styles for their wondrous productivity—for the assembly line and job standardization. But the hard-assed bosses of those days are fast becoming an endangered species. And now organizations' ambivalence toward their hierarchical structures is in full flower. Today authoritarian practices must be muted, not blared; disguised, not served up raw. Nevertheless, modern managers, like those of the past, have no choice except to impose controls and exercise some degree of authority—more politely than their forebears, perhaps, but still unmistakably.

The humanistic teachings and modifications of recent decades have certainly accomplished good work. They have helped many a struggling manager adapt to the fast-changing world. Yet, as a veteran executive once put it to one of my M.B.A. classes, "All organizations are prisons. It's just that the food is better in some than in others." The students didn't like that metaphor. They didn't want to think that they might be preparing for a career in the slammer.

Reaction: Oh, come on! That kind of do-it-or-else autocratic style went out with the Model T! We've long since learned all about morale and motivation. We don't treat people as "factors of production" any more. They're "human resources." We know we need their hearts and brains as well as their hands. People are our most important asset, and we don't kick our own assets.

Don't we? That's a response one might well hear topside, but not down in the engine room. Viewed from below, the authoritarian skyline remains clearly visible. If it is not, then why is Dilbert so popular? And why all the novels and films about greedy, selfish, dishonest, and otherwise toxic bosses? Why the hundreds, perhaps thousands, of corrective how-to books, leadership programs, and communications workshops that continue to pour down on students and middle managers everywhere?

It's harder than ever to find voices raised in hierarchies' defense. Instead we keep on denigrating them as despotic and irremediably flawed, the outdated progeny of absolute monarchies and rigid aristocracies. Hierarchies go on, but they also remain continuing fodder for cartoonists, novelists, and filmmakers. Invariably, they get taken for a ride.

A personal example: When some friends heard that I was starting a book on the *inevitability* of hierarchies, several of them were concerned that I might be writing a *defense* of hierarchies. They then turned peckish and accusatory, as though I were preparing to tout some evil variety of indentured servitude. They reject hierarchies because they dislike, as many of us do, the notion of some people forever telling others what to do. We don't cotton to forced dependency on others or others' forced dependency on us. That just doesn't feel right in our lands of the free.

ARE THEY INEVITABLE?

Again and again, over the years, many of us have wished, and some of us have believed, that a great white knight would come galloping out of the smog to slay the hierarchical dragon. In the wake of World War II, for example, many of us expected that the tsunami of newly arriving knowledge workers would sweep hierarchies away. Knowledge workers, after all, added value with their brains. Old authoritarian methods might work on arms and legs, but you couldn't push brains around. We were wrong. Many things changed, but hierarchies remained.

Later, in the 1970s, some of us felt sure that the new information revolution would drive a stake into the hierarchy's heart. For in the brave new IT world, every employee could gain instant access to all the information necessary to make informed decisions. Ergo, information would no longer have to flow tortuously up the hierarchy and decisions distortedly back down. Wrong again!

Now, in this era of cyberspace and nano-speed, that theme is recurring. Given today's knowledge world—its cheap, boundary-less communication, its interconnected organizations—who needs hierarchies? Some writers seem convinced that modern information technology—the Internet and the Web—have already killed hierarchies.

Thus, Thomas Stewart in his broad-ranging 1997 book *Intellectual Capital* tells us "How Technology Destroyed the Hierarchy."[7] And Stewart, it is worth pointing out, does not come at that end-of-hierarchies view from the usual, strictly humanistic posture. He is aware of what, in chapter 3, is called the "systemizing" perspective: a rational, analytic way of treating human organizations.

One must also ask another question: If networks are, in fact, the designs of the future, can we feel confident that they will do significantly better than hierarchies? We often fail to look down the road for the inevitable but unforeseen secondary and tertiary consequences of new "solutions" to today's problems—perhaps because we prefer not to face up to them in advance. As the great Eastern U.S. blackout of August 2003 made clear, interdependencies among a network of independent entities don't always prevent bad things from happening.[8] Networks, too, are subject to the vagaries of their weakest links and their most manipulative members.

Could it be that we have been fighting the wrong war? That organizational nirvana does not lie in battling against human hierarchies, but rather in learning to modify and tame them, and in helping people learn how to work effectively and live meaningfully inside them? Perhaps it's time to stop trying to persuade managers and other organizational employees to behave as though they are not occupants of authoritarian hierarchies, when, in fact, that's exactly where they live.

With these issues in mind, this book has three major goals. The first is to serve as a reality check, a reminder of what may be a bedrock fact of organizational life: that hierarchy is still, and is likely to remain, the foundational shape of almost every large, ongoing human organization.

The book's second goal is to look at hierarchies from the perspective of the large human organization. Why are new organizations still being designed hierarchically? What purposes—in our volatile new knowledge and informational world—does hierarchical architecture serve? How does its veiled but real authoritarian presence influence the life and work of the middle manager? Clearly hierarchies aren't what they used to be. But just how have they changed?

Have those changes been internally consistent and coherent? Have they made modern hierarchies more compatible with the aspirations of their people as well as the demands of their fast-changing environments?[9]

The book's third and most important purpose centers on supporting managers and the challenges they face. Although organizations have tried to digest the big changes thrust upon them by their volatile environments, many have been unable fully to integrate those changes. Tensions, gaps, and conflicts ensue. Some of the changes tend to drive organizations one way, while others push in the opposite direction. Often large hierarchical companies have "handled" such inconsistencies by simply off-loading them onto their middle managers, expecting these already overworked souls somehow to integrate and rationalize them. But how can middle managers do all that? How can they, for example, reconcile the softening, humanizing changes taking place in modern organizations with the simultaneous hardening, controlling changes brought on by modern information technology and by pressures for increasing speed? How can the men and women in the middle—balancing on the fragile rungs of hierarchical ladders—do their work amid today's roiling, multidirectional storms of change, and how can they find some sense of personal fulfillment while doing so?

Part One

THE INEVITABLE

HIERARCHY

*P*art I discusses why top-down orga-
nizational hierarchies, warts and all, are pretty much inevitable, and
why managers would do well to keep that reality in the forefront, and
not in the recesses, of their minds.

Chapter 1 looks at the negative sides of our attitudes toward hierarchies. Why have hierarchies become objects of so much fury and scorn?
What is it that many sensible people dislike about them, and why?
Chapter 2 examines why hierarchies persist despite all that hostility
and despite the rise of information technology, the Internet, the knowledge revolution, and the inventions of presumably better structural
forms. It looks first at the other side of the psychological coin: how those
of us who work inside hierarchies actually support and reinforce them,
even as we complain about them. Then the chapter examines some
earthly, practical reasons for the ubiquity of hierarchies—reasons associated, for example, with organizational size and efficiency.

ONE

Why We Don't Like Hierarchies

For decades, sensible people—management experts, educators, novelists, and more—have been fruitlessly attacking human hierarchies. Why? What's so terrible about hierarchies? Why do so many of us who work in hierarchies keep griping and complaining about them, but then go right on working in them, sometimes actually enjoying our work?

WHAT'S SO BAD ABOUT HIERARCHIES?

Why has *hierarchy* become a dirty word? The answers fall into many boxes, some emotional and otherwise psychological, and others rational and pragmatic. Here, first, are some of the more psychological ones.

They Generate Childlike Dependency

Dependency is built into human hierarchies. It follows necessarily from their pyramidal form. Like its close buddy, authority, dependency is an inescapable, immutable reality of hierarchical life. In human hierarchies, some people, by design, have more power than others, so those having less power become, to varying degrees, dependent on those having more.

Dependency is a human condition that always generates ambivalence and always causes complex emotional turmoil—a boiling mixture of love and hate, anger and fear, a tension driving toward both staying and fleeing. We need (and may much appreciate) what our organizations provide: our livelihoods, our key to the washroom, and our coveted corner office. But we don't like having to need such things. We want our freedom. We keep struggling to escape from dependency into freedom, and then we reverse course and fight to return to our protectors—as Erich Fromm put it, to "escape *from* freedom."[1] The hierarchies in which many of us spend much of our lives repel us, but they attract us, too. We want our jobs and all the other goodies hierarchies give us, but we also wish we didn't feel imprisoned by them. That dilemma can be infuriating.

One of my former professors used to give students a sense of dependency's essential qualities by asking us to imagine that we were the main character in a little story. He told it dramatically, in exquisite detail, until he had us squirming in empathy. Here's an abbreviated version of that story:

Imagine that you suffer from a strange disease. For as long as you can remember, you have been completely paralyzed. You can see, hear, think, and feel, but you can't move. Your malady, however, has one magical saving grace: When your older brother puts his hand on your shoulder, your paralysis disappears. (If you're a woman, make her a sister, but, for convenience, I'll keep the rest of this in the masculine form.) When he takes his hand away, however, you immediately drop back into paralysis.

Fortunately, your brother is a pretty nice guy. (You might also try this story with a not-so-nice brother or sister.) He keeps his hand on your shoulder as much as he can. But sometimes, of course, he must leave you for short periods.

Today, for example, Brother has a dental appointment across town. But before he goes, he helps you make yourself as comfortable as possible. It's a nice warm day, so you finish your coffee and sit down in a big easy chair by an open window. You can watch the action on the street below and get some fresh air, too. Before he goes, Brother turns on the radio to pleasant music. At 10 A.M. he leaves, promising to return by noon. Of course, you don't like this sort of thing, but it's only a couple of hours, and for you, that's life!

All goes well until about 10:30, when the radio program changes to very loud country music, the kind you really hate, and for some reason the volume on that old radio keeps increasing until the sound is pounding in your ears. There's also that button on the back of the chair, the one you've been meaning to fix but forgot about. It presses into your back in exactly the wrong place. By 11:00, the sky has clouded over, and it has begun to rain. A strong wind blows in. Soon you're soaked and cold. If you could shiver, you would. And why did you drink that extra cup of coffee? Your bladder is uncomfortably full.

Fortunately, you can see the clock. It's 11:45. Only fifteen minutes to go. You can stand the noise and the cold and the button in your back and the overloaded bladder for only fifteen little minutes.

But at noon, Brother still hasn't returned. You keep imagining you hear his car. 12:15 comes and goes, and 12:30. Now you're getting more than uncomfortable. You're getting worried, too. It's 12:45, then 1:00, and he's not back. You're not sure you can stand it much longer.

Then at 1:25, Brother comes waltzing in. "The dentist had an emergency," he says, as he takes off his coat. "I had to wait. I'm sorry. I'll be with you in a minute, after I rinse my mouth." Then he comes back and puts his hand on your shoulder.

This is the point at which our professor asked us two questions. "How would you *feel* when your brother finally put his hand back on your shoulder? And what would you *do?*" Of course we all knew what we'd do first. Head for the head. But how would we feel and what would we do after that? Some of us said we'd feel furious and we'd yell at Brother: "How could you do this to me? Don't you realize what you've put me through?" But then one of us would say, "That would be foolish. Yelling at him would just make him mad, and he might take his hand off and leave you hanging there with your mouth open and your fist in the air." Then somebody else would add, "Oh, I'd feel angry, of course, but I'd also feel grateful, thankful that he'd gotten home safely. What if he'd been in an accident or something? So even if I were wet and furious, I'd give him a big hug."

That's dependency and the ambivalence it generates: love and hate, anger and gratitude, a wish for release coupled with thankfulness that the key relationship is still intact. And although most of us who work in organizational hierarchies aren't paralyzed, we are, to a considerable extent, dependent on those up the hierarchy for our jobs, our income, and much of our status in the world. Brother hierarchy takes care of us, but we don't like needing his hand on our shoulder. As kids, we were dependent on our parents, and we both did and didn't like it. As aging parents we may, in turn, become dependent on our kids, and we will and won't like that, either. At work we're dependent on our bosses up the hierarchy, and we do and don't like that.

When one of my grandchildren was small, he summed up that dependency issue rather neatly. When his mother told him to do such-and-such, he asked, "Why do I have to?" His mother replied, "Because that's the rule." To which Marco responded, "How come you have all the rules and I don't have any?"

For those who work in hierarchies, ambivalence about dependency tends to be exacerbated by the contrast between life inside a company's walls and life on the outside. As free citizens of an open, democratic society, we have an inalienable right to complain, protest, and express our anger at bureaucratic injustice or stupidity—everywhere, that is, except at work. Neither managers nor their people have quite the same rights there. At work, from 9 to 5, the authoritarian hierarchy takes charge. There we must do what others have defined as our duties and responsibilities. We must meet their schedules, carry out their decisions, live in their décor, and abide by their dress codes. At 5, the gates swing open to release us back into freedom. Then, from 5 until 9 the next morning, we can make our own choices, decide our own meal times, decorate in our own tastes, and dress in our own styles.

That's an exaggeration, of course. It's a caricature. Nevertheless, the contrast between 9 to 5 and 5 to 9 is rather stark. The fact is that neither managers nor any other employees are hierarchies' *citizens.* We are hierarchies' dependent *employees.* Human relations experts keep trying, with only partial success, to make us into citizens of our work organizations. Most of that success, however, has resulted more from changes in attitude and style than from changes in hierarchical organizations' basic natures.

Hierarchies make us play by their authoritarian rules. They force us to obey and to be dependent, but, like Marco's mother, they also feed us and stroke us, so we need them. Ambivalence is thus especially maddening. If we could just plain hate our hierarchies, things would be fine. But to hate them and also need them? That's really infuriating! Perhaps that's what also makes us concoct mocking jokes and cartoons about the horrors of hierarchies. If we can't escape from hierarchies, at least we can—surreptitiously—stick our tongues out at them.

Perhaps if we lived in an autocratic society—in a dictatorship or an absolute monarchy—the relatively mild authoritarianism of our organizational hierarchies might pass unnoticed. Most of us might even accept obedience to higher authority as a "normal" way of life. Once, for example, in Soviet Leningrad, my wife and I waited in a long line of cars to buy gasoline. (We had already waited in a long line on the other side of town for coupons that would permit us to buy the gas.) A father and his small son waited in the car ahead of us. We began to chat in broken Russglish. I asked the father if he knew why we had to wait so long. He shrugged, smiled, and looked heavenward. "Because this is the Soviet Union," he replied.

We don't live in the Soviet Union. We don't just accept our dependency. We still get mad and fight back.

Organizations can certainly reduce the debilitating effects of their people's dependency, but they aren't likely to wipe it out—not until they wipe out hierarchies. And that's not likely to happen soon.

They Mistreat Us

We don't like big organizational hierarchies because they make working people unwilling serfs of stupid or wicked bosses. They shackle us to dull, repetitive routines. They discourage imagination. They quash creativity. They treat us capriciously. They make us do useless things. They don't really trust us, either. If they did, they wouldn't always be checking up on us. They throw us out into the cold whenever their stock prices drop. And that's only a short list of all the terrible things pyramid-shaped organizations do to people.

Yes, hierarchical organizations do such things. Just ask a random set of any large organization's employees, and they'll tell you stories you wouldn't want to hear. Of course, it's better now than it used to be—in some ways—but later in this book we'll get to some ways things have gotten worse, not better.

They Block Warm Interpersonal Relationships

We may be competitive animals, but we're also social critters. Three-quarters of a century ago, Harvard's Fritz Roethlisberger, after years of observational and experimental research at the Hawthorne Works of the Western Electric Company, noted the intensity of that social need:

> Whenever and wherever it was possible, [employees] generated [informal groups] like crazy. In many cases they found them so satisfying that they often did all sorts of non-logical things (that is, things that went counter to their economic interests) in order to belong to the small, warm, and cozy groups, which these relations generated. . . . The two kinds of relations were in sharp contrast. Among members of hierarchical relations, there were few interactions, few close friendships, and seldom any small, warm, cozy groups. There was sometimes "respect," but quite often distrust, apprehension, and suspicion. It was an unconscious battle between the logic of management and the sentiments of workers.[2]

In the past, many hierarchies actively discouraged such "warm, cozy" horizontal relationships. They preferred formal "hierarchical relations," in part because they were afraid that if their people got together, trouble would follow. But that's one place, isn't it, where many large hierarchies have changed over the past couple of decades? Teams and many other kinds of small groupings are now more likely to be encouraged actively in large hierarchies.

But has competition for individual stardom within those teams been actively *dis*couraged? Isn't this also one of the many ways in which hierarchies remain internally inconsistent? Aren't we still being thrown into the ring and forced to compete with our colleagues for raises and other prizes, while simultaneously being urged to be good team players? These tensions drag against interpersonal openness and trust.

Hierarchies are forever preaching about the importance of teamwork. But although they urge collaboration, they reward competition. They keep telling us we should cooperate with one another, and then they give only one of us the promotion. A friend of ours, a television actor, once won an Emmy award. After that, she told me, the solidarity of her show's cast just melted. Suddenly that hitherto collaborative and mutually supportive group split into fragments. "Why did *she* get the prize? Most of us were just as good as she was. And now Joe keeps bugging the writers for a more prominent part, so he, too, can get a shot at an Emmy."

Hierarchies shouldn't be able to have it both ways, but they do. They talk collaboration, but they're shaped like pyramids. They get narrower as we climb higher. Some people must be left behind.

They Breed Greed and Immorality

Despite all efforts to prevent recurrence of the high crimes of the past, many large modern hierarchies have certainly tolerated—even encouraged—massive greed and dishonesty. Hierarchies give some people great power, power that tends to build on itself. Eventually that power is likely to corrupt. Some of us seem unable to resist its siren song. And many of us start with positive ideals, only to have them erode as we struggle to make our way upward.[3]

The hierarchical form seems especially susceptible to power-mongering and chicanery. That troubling aspect of hierarchies came around at least once before in business organizations, back in the days of J. P. Morgan, Leland Stanford, and the other industrial "robber barons" of the early twentieth century. Now, given Enron, Andersen, World Com, Parmalat, Tyco, Adelphia, Warnaco, Global Crossing, and more, that issue has moved back into prominence. Later chapters will return to this scary aspect of many large hierarchies: their seductive promises of quick and easy wealth, promises that can attract the wrong people and drag even the right ones into venality.

SOME PRACTICAL ARGUMENTS AGAINST HIERARCHIES

Such humanistic reasons for wanting to get rid of hierarchies aren't the only ones that can be marshaled. Here are some more practical, more "rational" reasons.

They're Inefficient

Hierarchies' purported inefficiencies loom large: the communication failures within the CIA before 9/11, the Pentagon's misreadings of Vietnam, the supposed inability of big bureaucracies to innovate, and the endless tales of in-company screwups and scandals regularly recounted in the *WSJ*, *BusinessWeek*, *Fortune*, and *The Economist*.

Most of us have our own pet horror stories about the wastefulness and inefficiency of hierarchies. Here's one from a former member of President Jimmy Carter's domestic policy staff.[4]

> *Late one Friday afternoon the word came down: The president absolutely, positively needed a detailed report about Problem X by 8:00 Monday morning.*
>
> *Could anything be more important? How about your ten-year-old's birthday party scheduled for tomorrow? Or that long-delayed weekend visit to your sick mother? Trivial by comparison! All canceled. A few minutes of apologetic phone calls to unhappy children, spouses, and friends, then get to work on that terribly important report.*
>
> *Everyone pitches in. They work until after midnight on Friday, late into the night on Saturday, and again on Sunday, assembling and reviewing data, rechecking numbers, organizing, debating, and rewriting conclusions. Food? Chinese take-out and coffee.*
>
> *The goal is clear. So is the deadline. The group is hot. They give it everything they've got. And they do it! Early Monday morning the completed report, bound and beautiful, sits on the Oval Office desk.*

Exhilaration prevails, coupled with camaraderie. Getting a tough job done does that to groups. It heats them up, stirs the blood.

Then, on Monday, the group awaits acknowledgment from on high. But none comes. Nor is there any news on Tuesday, nor on Wednesday.

It turns out, of course, that the president didn't *need* that report. He had simply remarked—in the presence of some staff members—that he would like to see how Problem X was doing. So the group's masterwork sat buried in a pile, waiting for the moment when he might glance at it.

Such snowballs of misinformation are commonplace in large hierarchies. They grow, distort, and accelerate as they roll down bureaucratic pyramids. Casual comments become suggestions. Suggestions metamorphose into orders from the boss. Orders upgrade to commands, and commands to crises. Crises are great motivators of action, but repeated false cries of "fire" are also great motivators of *re*action. The president, high above it all, surely had no idea that he, via the hierarchy, had just taken a giant step toward converting a loyal, dedicated team into cynical bureaucrats.

One can explain away this episode as just another example of fouled-up governmental bureaucracy. But we have all seen such scenarios played out in large organizations everywhere. In the old days at General Electric, for example, it used to be said that whenever the CEO asked for a cup of coffee, an employee went out and tried to buy Brazil.[5] A comparable tale about Henry J. Kaiser still occasionally circulates through the corridors of Kaiser Permanente. Mr. Kaiser liked fresh fruits and vegetables, so once, before departing on an extended trip, he announced that he would just love to have his own vegetable garden. Somehow, that request got lost until two days before his scheduled return. Because Mr. Kaiser also liked his orders carried out, a disaster loomed. A huge team of gardeners was hastily summoned. For two days and two nights they plowed and planted. When Henry J. returned, he beamed at his neat, weedless new garden. Obviously pleased, so the legend goes, he pulled up a perfect, full-grown carrot—unaware that it had been planted there the night before.

We all know that such silly things happen in large organizations, but far worse things also happen. These massive institutions can be terribly wasteful of talent, and cruel, and quite stupid, too—despite their considerate and intelligent occupants. Given their pervasive twin shortcomings—inhumanity and apparent inefficiency—it is no wonder that we keep looking for alternatives. But do you know of any more efficient architectures? Are there other feasible organizational designs that would build large numbers of reliable and steadily better airplanes or computers or kitchen sinks? Structures that would, by their natures, operate both more efficiently and more humanely?

They're Slow, Unresponsive, and Inflexible

Hierarchies crawl, ponderously, while lively smaller organizations dance around them, nipping at their heels. Hierarchies are rigid, unimaginative, and uncreative.

Are those stereotypes true? Certainly not. As others have shown, and as we shall try to show later, many big "dinosaurs" have proven themselves quite agile, flexible, adaptive, and even innovative.[6] IBM? Nokia? Mitsubishi? GE? Intel? Younger giants such as Amazon.com and Dell? If these and other big hierarchies can do it, maybe it's not their basic hierarchical architecture that's to blame for the failings of others.

Actually, large size gives the big old organizations an advantage, even when it comes to things we usually associate with small size. Big hierarchies are *big*. This means that they can be slow *and* fast, rigid *and* flexible, stodgy *and* adaptive at the same time. Big organizations can afford to take many small (for them) risks and have several of them fail. Think of how much less dangerous it is for a large hierarchy to bet on the same long shot experiment as a small start-up. For the big company, the experiment risks only a small portion of its total resources. For the little one, the long shot may be its one shot.

They Violate Democratic Values

Large organizations' inescapable need for hierarchy, and therefore for authority, clashes with egalitarian values of democratic societies. Their requirement that we must never forget who's boss—even when we're boss—continues to trouble many of us. It simply doesn't fit with *liberté, egalité, fraternité*. This mismatch is an ongoing irritant. Organizational hierarchies are just not democracies. We can slow down organizations' authoritarian train and keep trying to slow it further. We can de-emphasize authoritarianism and disguise it, but we are unlikely to bring it to a halt.

Organizations need humanism and the creativity, energy, and imagination of motivated people, but they also need hierarchical structure and the control and accountability that attach to it. These opposing twins are as vital to large organizations as the twins of autonomy and self-discipline are to the individual.

They Don't Like Us

While many of us keep trying to get hierarchies off our backs, hierarchies keep trying to get us humans off theirs. Hierarchies would surely wish (if they could wish) that they could get rid of us. Think how much more smoothly those giants would run if they could get along without all the complaining and demanding and loafing we humans do. We're forever showing up late for work, or making terrible errors, or quitting without notice, or calling in sick, or filching the company's pencils, or using its computers for personal purposes.

Of course, big hierarchical organizations swear up and down that they love us. They throw company barbecues, and they supply the booze at holiday parties. They come up with PR mantras such as "People are our most important asset." But take care! Just as some of us are forever trying to find alternatives to hierarchies, hierarchies always have an eye out for alternatives to us. They're pouncing on every new technology they can find that might help them get rid of us unreliable, trouble-making "human resources."

The dependency issue recurs here, but in reverse. We are dependent on hierarchies, but hierarchies are also dependent on us. We cozy up to our organizations because we need our jobs, but our organizations also cozy up to us because they need our arms, legs, and, occasionally, our brains. The dependency is reciprocal, but the power is usually one-sided.

A second oddity: We humans keep trying to shake free of hierarchies' grasp, but we also actively resist when they try to free us. Beginning way back, we have waged an unrelenting battle to preserve our right to work in those structures we profess to hate. And we fight hardest when they are about to release us.

Even for the Boss, They Have Big Downsides

We can easily forget, as we consider hierarchical organizations' human failings, that people on the lower rungs aren't their only victims. Those at the top may reap great benefits, but they too must pay a share of hierarchies' human costs. To maintain power, leaders of hierarchies must also distribute power. Distributing power, a.k.a. authority, can be dangerous, especially vis-à-vis the emperor's immediate entourage. Confidants and cronies close to the top can, and often do, use their delegated power to foment intrigues and conspiracies. Kings, sultans, presidents, and CEOs must therefore pay for their power in the currency of personal security. From Julius Caesar to modern corporate chieftains, powerful leaders have been brought down, not by enemies from without, but by their own backstabbing aides. Add the fact that leaders can seldom escape the spotlight, a spotlight that may bring unwelcome attention and even physical danger along with glory and stardom. In Italy, senior executives worry about their kneecaps. In Mexico, many carefully vary their routes to and from work. Saddam Hussein, like the Russian czars, slept in a different palace each night. Shakespeare got it right: "Uneasy lies the head that wears a crown."

That pinnacle position is loaded with psychological as well as physical dangers. Hierarchies repeatedly infect their leaders with horrendous mental illnesses. Holding the seat atop the pyramid can trigger delusions of omnipotence, cruel and dreadful searches for immortality, and paranoid fears of nonexistent enemies. The first emperor of China built his enormous terra cotta armies to ensure his power in the afterworld. He sent boatloads of children on one-way trips to sea in search of his imagined islands of immortality. Saddam Hussein's iron heel was intended to guarantee his legacy and his family's continuing riches. Chairman Mao, late in life, felt a need to maintain his power by instituting his quite insane cultural revolution. So although hierarchies can glorify their leaders, they can also twist them into terrified and terrifying near-psychotics, especially when they have been in power too long.

It is for such reasons—some rational, others irrational—that hierarchies continue to haunt our lives, even as they replenish them.

IN SUMMARY

Dependency, this chapter has suggested, is the key to much of our dislike of hierarchical organizations and much of the reason we also cling to them. Dependency generates ambivalence. Paradoxically, we would probably like hierarchies better if we could just plain hate them. But we can't. The plus side of our ambivalence keeps poking through our protests. We hate hierarchies and wish they would go away, but we want them to go on taking care of us. That mix is vexing, especially because hierarchies feel the same way about us. They wish we would go away, but, for now, difficult human beings are their most precious resource. What a relationship! It's much like some painful marriages. He and she can't stand each other, but they can't do without each other.

It's not only our dependency that makes us dislike hierarchies. Those of us who work in them complain for many other reasons. Writers and cartoonists caricature hierarchies as stupid or cruel or screwed up. Serious students of organizations make similar assessments and provide evidence to support their claims. Those anti-hierarchical plaints fall into at least four categories. First, hierarchies are inhumane. Second, they are inefficient. Third, they are anti-democratic. Fourth, they are breeders of immorality. Each of those protestations has some, but not total, validity and none is the least bit likely to cause us to outlaw hierarchies, even if we knew how—and even if we really wanted to.

Chapter 2 identifies some reasons we don't kill off hierarchies. It looks at the upside of our ambivalence; why and how we humans help to keep hierarchies going, and why we support and encourage them even as we wage war against them. It also points to some hard-headed, practical reasons for the ubiquity of hierarchies.

TWO

Why Hierarchies
Persist

If hierarchies have so many human and productive failings, why are they still with us? Organizational hierarchies, after all, are built and populated by humans. Yet even in our democratic societies and in our high-tech information age, we not only put up with hierarchies but also keep adding new ones. And why do many of us free, autonomous human beings spend much of our lives incarcerated in these pyramid-shaped torture chambers?

Why pyramids? Why don't we reshape our organizations into, say, cylinders, or soccer balls, or fishing nets, or circles? At least one sensible effort has been made in that last, circular direction, and although it has been tried in a few organizations, it, like many other experimental forms, has never come close to replacing the hierarchy.[1]

DON'T BLAME HIERARCHIES ON BAD GUYS

Here is one easy answer to the "why hierarchies?" question, but it won't fly. Let's blame the rich and powerful! Hierarchies are there to help them become richer and more powerful. The pharaohs of Egypt built their great pyramids to guarantee their power in the next life. Modern pharaohs, some people feel, build organizational pyramids for that same paranoid purpose. Captains of industry construct great human pyramids to house their power-driven egos and to ensure their legacies, along with immense here-and-now earthly rewards. Huge hierarchies are nothing more than the "immortality projects" of modern organizational emperors.[2]

For some cynical critics, that's the obvious answer. Isn't every dictatorship a tightly controlling hierarchy? Haven't steep hierarchies always characterized absolute monarchies? And aren't giant organizational hierarchies simply their contemporary equivalents? "Egotistical leadership and autocratic decision making" have not departed our new world.

In these days of self-serving CEOs, that old jeremiad may even contain a modicum of merit. But it's not a very solid argument. Absent rapacious, power-hungry CEOs, would corporate hierarchies just skulk away? Not likely. Greed and power hunger certainly contribute their bits to the support of human hierarchies. It's true, too, that those who have lots of power usually want to keep it, and that many leaders have exploited their hierarchies for selfish ends.

Notice, however, that we can make a stronger case for the reverse argument. Instead of blaming hierarchies on bad guys, let's blame bad guys on hierarchies. Power does indeed tend to corrupt. And once ensconced on the pinnacle of a large hierarchy, few top executives are willing voluntarily to climb down.

But bad guys are far from the heart of the matter. Some good guys at the top have managed to maintain their integrity despite hierarchy's corrupting influence. Indeed hierarchies are not the exclusive property of *any* guys, good or bad. They are, as we shall try to show, just as ubiquitous in many other systems as in human systems, even in systems that have *no* guys.

Here, then, are some other, perhaps more realistic answers to the question of why human hierarchies persist, and why even people like you and me continue to work in them. So, this time, Mr. or Ms. Manager, think about the *positives* of your job, things such as pay and Christmas parties, but also deeper, underlying things. What, if anything, do *you* get out of working in a big hierarchical organization?

HIERARCHIES LET US FEED OUR FAMILIES

We put up with many of the downsides of hierarchical organizations simply because we need our jobs. Of course, even if the organizations that employ us weren't hierarchical, we would still want to keep our jobs. But they *are* hierarchical, and one reason we tolerate the pain they cause is simply because they pay us. In 2002, according to a Conference Board survey, roughly half of American employees didn't like their jobs, and the percentage was rising, not falling.[3] Still, we don't want those fountains of funds to dry up. We may protest, organize unions, pass laws, and in a multitude of other ways try to hold organizational hierarchies at bay, but we don't really want to kill them. It's that old ambivalence and dependency again, this time with a practical side. We toil in hierarchical organizations because we like to eat. We may reluctantly accept pay cuts when our organizations are in trouble, as pilots and others did to help keep their airlines alive after 9/11. The alternative, joblessness, is a lot less fun than a job we don't like.

HIERARCHIES MEET OUR PSYCHOLOGICAL NEEDS

We gripe about hierarchies, but we try hard to get ourselves accepted into them. That makes us, in a sense, hierarchies' willing co-conspirators. It's true that some of us are occasionally shanghaied into organizations against our wills. Remember your first day at school? Staying home with Mother and your stuffed animals would have been much nicer. And if, as a young adult, you were drafted into the military, your first day in the barracks wasn't much fun either.

But during most of our lives, we are neither dragged off to school nor dragooned into the Navy. More often we try, quite actively, to get ourselves admitted to the university or hired at Starbucks or BP or Honda or Citibank. We volunteer to work in hierarchies, and so do many others. And after we get in, we don't try very hard to get out. We may move from one hierarchy to another, but few of us choose to opt out of the whole system.

Hierarchies Provide Ladders to Climb

Hierarchies offer us an achievement ladder to climb, a clearly de-marcated route toward status and wealth. When we finish school—that's one hierarchy—most of us look for a job in another, for a place where we can "get ahead." Hierarchies provide markers of upward progress. In hierarchies, clerks can climb to become department heads, corporals to become sergeants, and parish priests to become bishops. Hierarchies are major arenas in which we play out our achievement needs.

The theme of individual achievement is perhaps particularly central in our classic American saga. It's a tale told to us again and again by America's tribal elders. Abe Lincoln summed it up in the 1850s:

> *There is no permanent class of hired laborers among us. The pru-dent, penniless beginner in the world labors for wages awhile, saves a surplus with which to buy tools or land for himself, and at length hires another new beginner to help him. If any continue through life in the condition of the hired laborer, it is not the fault of the sys-tem, but because of either a dependent nature that prefers it, or improvidence, folly, or singular misfortune.*[4]

Nowadays, Lincoln's admonishments are hard to follow. The ratio of reality to myth in that now multinational saga has changed. Many of us do continue through life in the condition of a "hired laborer." But Lincoln's ideal of independence is still real enough to inspire and encourage us to clamber up hierarchical pyramids, and still real enough in many industrialized nations to bring eager immigrants swarming to their shores.

Not all societies weave that achievement story into their cultural fabric. Some send their young the message that it is only through sheer luck that one can hope to move up. In others, family ties or connections, and not hard work, are the main routes. But in modern-day democracies, most of us are taught to want to climb, and hierarchies provide convenient ladders.

But which way is up? The relationship between hierarchies and the human need for achievement is worth further exploration. For one thing, many of us don't begin at the bottoms of hierarchies any more. We go for our B.A.'s or M.B.A.'s first and then enter on a middle rung of the ladder to success. And others, such as some in the professions, prefer to climb atypical ladders. Many scientists and technologists, for example, would not view a "promotion" to an administrative job as a real promotion. Bell Laboratories in its glory days was so sensitive about that issue that its top executives always made sure a scientist occupied the chief administrative officer's chair. They did it to ensure that the scientific side of the house remained in control of the organization's definition of achievement and that the administrative side stayed the junior partner in establishing the criteria of success.

Academic hierarchies are also somewhat atypical. In American universities as well as those of some other nations, there are only three professorial ranks. Young academics can move from assistant professor to associate and finally to tenured full professor, a rank that many reach by about the age forty. Full professors then usually remain at that rank for another thirty years. There *is* no higher rank. Once tenured, professors can't be fired unless they do something egregious. As for salary, it may increase slowly, but there are no stock options or other quick fixes, except perhaps the royalties from a rare best-selling book. Of course, a professor can certainly aspire to a deanship or a college presidency. But these would likely be seen as transfers out of the academic and into the administrative hierarchy, from one achievement ladder to an entirely different one.

Once they're tenured, then, with no higher rungs to climb and another three decades to go, what "motivates" such people? Do full professors just hang around the faculty club and keep reusing their ten-year-old lecture notes? Yes, one or two may do exactly that. The overwhelming majority don't. They, too, have been bitten by the achievement bug, so—helped along by some peer pressures—they build their own ladders. They keep right on working to solve their interesting (sometimes interesting only to themselves) problems and the problems born of those problems and the problems born of those. The markers of progress up those semiprivate ladders are seldom well defined, but they can be highly attractive.

Multiple achievement ladders are quite consistent with our meritocratic parable. "Work hard, young person, and no matter your origin or pedigree, you too can reach the top." That story remains largely true. Hard and good work really does help us climb ladders to success. Hierarchies are also quite consistent with a more worrisome corollary, the notion that success *deserves* to be one's primary life goal. Organizational hierarchies operationalize that idea. They provide clear signposts along the way up. Promotions, raises, bonuses, stock options, and a variety of perquisites all serve as brightly illuminated signals for those who choose to make such success their top priority. And few of us, even today, dispute the basic righteousness of this entire achievement orientation.

Hierarchies Help Us Define Ourselves

A job in a hierarchical organization provides something far more vital than the chance to climb. Like our families, communities, and religions, our jobs give us identity, a flag to fly. Our positions in hierarchies help establish our place in the world—and each of us requires a place. One need only scan the obituaries in today's newspaper to see how much we are defined by our positions in hierarchies. These positions tell the world—and ourselves—that we are *somebody*, not *nobody*.[5]

Here's a pop quiz: Write down—quickly, off the top of your head—three short answers to this question: Who are you?

Do any of your answers have to do with your place in a hierarchical organization?

Think of how it *feels* to be pushed out of your position in your hierarchy, to be demoted, or to be out of a job for months and months. Loss of income is only part of the problem, and often a small part. Self-esteem is involved here—one's role in society, one's very identity. In our individualistic, go-get-'em culture, joblessness is almost sinful. It takes a strong ego for someone who is unemployed to hang on to a sense of self-worth. Executives who have been involuntarily released must construct bravely defensive cover stories as they hunt for new jobs. They know that potential employers may perceive them, simply because they are out of work, as rootless, powerless, even unworthy of respect. Only the very young and the very old are permitted the luxury of respectable joblessness. And for the very old, it is still important to make sure that the world knows you *have been* a division director at BP or a manager at Starbucks or a professor at Stanford. We cling to hierarchies because our place in a hierarchy is, rightly or wrongly, a major indicator of our social worth.

For many of us, and perhaps especially for Americans, our jobs have become even more than an indicator of who we are. They have become the central focus of our lives. In 2000, we Americans worked approximately three hundred fifty hours more per year than Europeans.[6] That's almost nine more forty-hour weeks. In the current state of the world, this centrality of work can hardly be considered desirable. As Joanne Ciulla has pointed out, "Of all the institutions in society, why would we let one of the more precarious ones supply our social, spiritual, and psychological needs? It doesn't make sense to put such a large portion of our lives into the unsteady hands of employers."[7]

Big Hierarchies Grant Us an Illusion of Security

Hierarchies provide the welcome, albeit spurious, illusion that they will shelter and protect us from the wild winds of the turbulent world. Other architectures might do the same, but it's hierarchies that are there and doing it. That illusion is part of the plus side of dependency.

This security blanket isn't quite as secure as it used to be. Nevertheless, a seemingly solid job in a large organization is still a powerful way to reassure ourselves that we are safe; that we have our place to go to each morning, that our regular paychecks will continue to arrive, tomorrow and tomorrow. Snuggled into Mother Hierarchy's ample bosom, our personhood is affirmed and our existential angst allayed. At least that was the way it felt for many of us, until, as on 9/11/01, the indestructible is destroyed or Enron explodes and Andersen falls apart. Then reality sets in, and with it the realization that we may have taken too many good things for granted.

Hierarchies Add Structure to Our Lives

Jobs in hierarchies make our lives orderly. They provide routines and regularity. We need such things. A friend of mine, after he retired, took to keeping goats. "Why goats?" I once asked him. "You're a city boy. I didn't think you knew a goat from a sheep."

"I keep goats," he replied, "because goats have to be milked regularly. They give me a reason to wake up every morning."

My friend, like most of us, needed to be needed. His company no longer needed him, so he searched for something that did: goats. Without them he might have found himself, like many retirees, afloat in a sea of anomie.

Some leaders, including many less-than-lovable ones, exploit this need to be needed. They understand that although hierarchies' demand for conformity frustrates some human needs, it simultaneously satisfies others, including needs for structure and membership. These social needs manifest themselves all around us, in our clubs, fraternities and sororities, associations, amateur teams, and a thousand other groupings. It was the young Frenchman Alexis de Tocqueville, in his classic *Democracy in America,* who long ago pointed to the propensity of Americans to form groups of all kinds, everywhere, and at the drop of a hat.[8] Indeed, if we check the Web for information about de Tocqueville, we find an American voluntary organization whose central purpose is simply to celebrate de Tocqueville. That propensity to organize is surely no longer exclusively American. It now seems to be happening in more or less democratic societies everywhere.

Hierarchies Evaluate Us

Hierarchies evaluate us. They tell us how good or bad we are and whether we are getting better or worse. These evaluations are often invalid and even more often unjust. Nevertheless, we want to be evaluated—a bald assertion that will surely raise some hackles.

How can this guy say we *want* to be evaluated? I *hate* being evaluated. At school they marked us (that's the right word, *marked;* they marked us for life!) on a curve, so even if we all worked hard, some of us had to flunk. Now, in the company, they evaluate us in quartiles, so no matter how hard people at the lower end try, they'll probably stay in the fourth quartile. I hate that part of my job. It's painful to be evaluated, and even more painful to feed back negative evaluations to someone else. Somehow this whole evaluating thing just doesn't feel right. We want to be evaluated? Baloney! Next thing you know they'll want parents to evaluate their kids—on a curve!

Many of us feel pretty much that way. We aren't comfortable with the notion that some people should have the right to decide on the worth of other people. That decision belongs to God, not to my company's assistant vice-president.

We do all sorts of things to avoid getting (or giving) *negative* evaluations. In U.S. companies, griping about performance appraisals is almost a national pastime. Those evaluations, especially those with the merest hint of negativity, generate wails of protest from evaluators as well as evaluatees. Try asking professors what they hate even more than grading papers. Answer: having to listen to students' complaints about their grades. Supervisors find all kinds of ways to delay or finesse appraisal feedback interviews. Back in the Navy, average "fitness report" ratings gradually climbed so high that we were trying to differentiate between 98s and 99s out of 100.

Maybe that's why HR people seem to come up with, annually, with new, guaranteed painless appraisal techniques. This year's version promises, the memo says, to increase validity and remove all stress from the process. But these nostrums never quite do the job. So the howling continues.

How, then, can any right-minded person assert that we *want* to be evaluated? Here's an answer: People have achievement needs. On that dimension, managers, from supervisors to CEOs, are probably in the top decile of their nations' populations. Humans are competitive, too, especially males. Twenty years of research on achieving styles with more than twenty thousand male and female managers from around the world comes up with only one consistent difference between the sexes. Men everywhere score higher on competitiveness (one of nine achieving styles) than women. But women *managers* score higher on competitiveness than non-managerial women.[9] Managers, that is, are competitors, and competitors *want* yardsticks. Joe wants to know that he's smarter than Mary or a better marketer than Sam. Our egos want report cards. We want to be measured, evaluated, even if those measures are imperfect and seldom make us happy. The one thing that may well generate even more fury than an existing evaluation procedure would be to have no evaluation procedure at all.

Organizational hierarchies, furthermore, have no choice except to evaluate. A pyramid becomes narrower as one approaches its top. That design requires organizations to select and cull. They must justify their decisions about how to distribute pay, promotions, and other rewards. So they take their questionable measurements seriously and promote people and allocate raises and bonuses accordingly. That's the fair way, isn't it? Much better than promoting you because you're the boss's son-in-law. And even though we grouch and grumble, most of us buy into that evaluation game.

Hierarchies Fit Our Individual-Oriented Society

The United States, like many other countries, is not just an achieving society; it is an *individual-centered* achieving society.

Such an assertion may sound silly. For example, how can military hierarchies, which demand lockstep conformity, be "individual-centered"? Armies (and some companies, too) do everything they can to *de*-individualize their recruits. They give them all the same haircuts and dress them all in the same uniforms to encourage uniformity and to suppress individuality.

Hierarchies are *not* consistent with individualism, nor are they with individuality. The military and most other hierarchical organizations tend to clobber both of these. Yet hierarchical architecture is quite consistent with the cultural belief that it is each individual's duty to make her own way—*as long as she plays by the organization's rules*. Hierarchies provide an ideal arena for individual achievement even as they demand conformity. Indeed, they make conformity nearly a precondition for achievement. With few exceptions, individuals must first conform to community standards before being permitted to show their individual stuff.

Hierarchical organizations are the perfect diamonds on which to play out the common values we learned in childhood. They set the rules of the game. They provide all the bases. They demarcate the foul lines. And they keep score on our every hit, run, and error. In fact, American baseball may be just the right metaphor for characterizing our society's simultaneous support of both conformity to group standards and individual merit. The late Bart Giamatti, ex-president of Yale University and ex-commissioner of American major league baseball, eloquently described that mix:

> *Baseball fits America so well because it embodies the interplay of individual and group that we so love, and because it expresses our longing for the rule of law while licensing our resentment of lawgivers. Baseball, the opportunist's game, puts a tremendous premium on the individual . . . And while the premium on individual effort is never lost, the communal choreography of the team eventually takes over . . . The subsequent interactions among all the players on the field expand in incalculable ways. When in the thrall of these communal aspects, hitting, stealing a base, and individual initiative give way to collective playmaking, acts of sacrifice or cooperation . . . Whether on offense or defense, the virtuoso is subsumed into the ensemble.*[10]

It's the best individual players—the ones who conform to the common standards—whom we admire most, but occasionally a great athlete turns out to be non-conforming; not a team player. Then we must walk the tightrope between admiration and disapproval, as baseball fans did with such outstanding but "difficult" figures as Ted Williams, Roger Maris, and, especially, Ty Cobb. Even as I write this, a firestorm of debate encircles Pete Rose, champion hitter but admitted liar and illicit gambler.

HIERARCHIES PERSIST FOR PRAGMATIC REASONS

So far this chapter has offered mostly psychological reasons for hierarchies' perseverance. We humans support hierarchies because they satisfy many of our needs and ameliorate many of our anxieties. But how did hierarchies get there in the first place? Who or what put them there? If we didn't support them, would they disappear? Not a chance. They're much too useful to abandon. Down-to-earth, pragmatic forces give birth to hierarchies and keep helping to reinvigorate them.

There are at least two kinds of such pragmatic forces. The first is efficiency. Hierarchies remain the standard in large organizations simply because they are efficient. Don't laugh! Hierarchies are really quite efficient, and competitive managerial types set much store by efficiency. The second is a pair of forces: size and age. These two—pressures for efficiency, plus growth and aging—keep converting new non-hierarchies into hierarchies and keep protecting old hierarchies from their predatory enemies.

Hierarchies Are Efficient

If large business organizations are to survive in our competitive milieu, they must at least approximate the efficiency of their competitors. Hierarchical design helps them to become efficient enough to get their complicated work done. If their competitors had discovered other, more efficient non-hierarchical forms, most hierarchies wouldn't still be hierarchies.

That's not to say that hierarchies are *highly* efficient. They're more akin to Winston Churchill's characterization of democracy: Hierarchy may be the worst form of organization—except for all the others. For large, complicated human organizations, they're the best wheel—perhaps the only feasible wheel—in town.

The assertion that the hierarchical form is efficient will surely cause many readers to roll their eyes heavenward. Any employee of any large hierarchy can regale you with tales of its inefficiencies—of delays, distortions, and foul-ups. Nevertheless, despite barrels full of waste, redundancies, and omissions, hierarchical systems are effective structures for getting big, complex jobs done, especially when compared with available alternatives.

So before that efficiency argument makes you quit this book in disgust, please take a moment to read this excerpt from one of Rudyard Kipling's rhythmic, late nineteenth-century colonial tales. It's a rare paean of praise for hierarchies, and it provides one pragmatic answer to the basic question of why hierarchies persist.

The story, called "Her Majesty's Servants," describes a great pageant staged by the viceroy of India to impress a visiting amir from Afghanistan.[11] Thousands of troops, thirty marching bands, and countless draft animals have been assembled to help mount this colorful, awe-inspiring spectacle. Late in the story, this exchange takes place:

> *Then I heard an old, grizzled, longhaired Central Asian chief, who had come down with the Amir, asking questions of a native officer.*
>
> *"Now," he said, "In what manner was this wonderful thing done?"*
>
> *And the officer answered, "An order was given and they obeyed."*
>
> *"But are the beasts as wise as the men?" said the chief.*
>
> *"They obey, as the men do. Mule, horse, elephant, or bullock, he obeys his driver, and the driver his sergeant, and the sergeant his lieutenant, and the lieutenant his captain, and the captain his major, and the major his colonel, and the colonel his brigadier commanding three regiments, and the brigadier the general, who obeys the Viceroy, who is the servant of the Empress. Thus it is done."*
>
> *"Would it were so in Afghanistan," said the chief, "for there we obey only our own wills."*
>
> *"And for that reason," said the native officer, twirling his mustache, "your Amir whom you do not obey must come here and take orders from our Viceroy."*

Of course that dramatic demonstration of the hierarchy's effectiveness has its second side. Shouldn't one also feel some empathy for that "old, grizzled, longhaired chief?" Unlike the colonial officer, he's not just another link in a long chain of command. He's an autonomous human being, beholden to no will but his own. Would he have sacrificed his autonomy for all the hierarchical discipline of the British Raj? Indeed in that respect, the Afghan's creed is actually very close to the Western creed of individualism—a philosophy, in fact, that presents a perennial organizational challenge for business leaders. It's also worth noting that although the well-organized, hierarchical British tried repeatedly in the nineteenth century, they never succeeded in controlling badly organized Afghanistan. Nor did the Soviets in the late twentieth century. Nor, at this writing, have the Americans in the early twenty-first.

Does Kipling's description mean that everything went smoothly in the planning and execution of that impressive military show? Surely not. The preparation and implementation must have been replete with the usual glitches, last-minute crises, overbearing officers, wrong units in the wrong places at the wrong times, and all the other headaches and natural shocks that hierarchies are heir to. But it worked. And from the outside looking in, it worked with wondrous efficiency.

ARE THERE HIERARCHIES IN OUR HEADS?

The efficiency argument may not impress some readers. It may remind others of the obsessive "efficiency men" of long ago. But the fact is that we are all efficiency men and women. The first time we play tic-tac-toe, it's fun, but only for a few rounds, until we get it all programmed in our heads. Then the game becomes rather boring. Yet most of us can't keep ourselves from programming it. Nor can we keep ourselves from programming other initially ill-structured problems.

We humans, after all, aren't just emotional, feeling creatures. We also think. But most of the grievances we hold against human hierarchies are about the terrible things they do to our feelings. They frustrate, anger, and demean us. They treat us unfairly, bore us, and push us around.

Cognitively, however—intellectually—hierarchies help more than they harm. The thinking parts of us humans must look upon hierarchies quite favorably because we opt for them almost automatically. Why? It's because they're sensible tools for simplifying complicated problems.

Some of the good sense of hierarchical thinking is captured succinctly in this simple-sounding metaphor once put forward by Nobelist Herbert Simon:

There once were two watchmakers, named Hora and Tempus, who manufactured very fine watches. Both of them were highly regarded, and the phones in their workshops rang frequently—new customers were constantly calling them. However, Hora prospered, while Tempus became poorer and poorer and finally lost his shop. What was the reason?

The watches the men made consisted of about 1,000 parts each. Tempus had so constructed his that if he had one partly assembled and had to put it down—to answer the phone, say—it immediately fell to pieces and had to be reassembled from the elements. The better the customers liked his watches, the more they phoned him and the more difficult it became for him to find enough uninterrupted time to finish each watch.

The watches that Hora made were no less complex than those of Tempus. But he had designed them so that he could put together subassemblies of about ten elements each. Ten of these subassemblies, again, could be put together into a larger subassembly; and a system of ten of the latter subassemblies constituted the whole watch. Hence, when Hora had to put down a partly assembled watch to answer the phone, he lost only a small part of his work, and he assembled his watches in only a fraction of the man-hours it took Tempus.[12]

Simon then goes on to do the numbers:

Now if p *is about 0.01—that is, there is one chance in a hundred that either watchmaker will be interrupted while adding any one part to an assembly—then a straightforward calculation shows that it will take Tempus on the average about four thousand times as long to assemble a watch as Hora.*[13]

Of course, both Tempus and Hora are now out of business— Tempus because of the not-very-sensible way he built watches, and Hora because he had made enough money to retire comfortably before being displaced by the arrival of electronic watches.

Tempus, one must conclude, really needed help. He just couldn't have been very bright. But neither did Hora have to be an Einstein to figure out his more efficient method. Wouldn't 99 percent of us have learned, all by ourselves, to do about the same thing—to build those watches hierarchically? In fact, our use of hierarchical approaches to problems is so common in our everyday lives that one must consider the possibility that hierarchical thinking may somehow be hard-wired into the human brain (Tempus's brain excepted). The common use of hierarchies to assemble bits and pieces seems to be one part of what we mean by "common sense."

My mother must have believed that. When I was five or six years old, I would sometimes lose a button from my shirt. So Mama would sit in her favorite chair with her sewing basket, and I would stand in front of her while she sewed on a new button. But before she took the first stitch, she always insisted that I put my thumb in my mouth. That was to make sure, she told me, that she would not inadvertently sew up my *shachel*—my common sense. Tempus's mother must have sewn on his buttons *sans* thumb-in-mouth. Indeed, if we humans have any innate cognitive abilities, they must surely include the *shachel* to figure out that hierarchies are pretty good ways to do lots of things.

Hora's hierarchies are not the human hierarchies that this book is mostly about. His hierarchies didn't involve hundreds of people stacked up in multi-tiered pyramids. People-free hierarchies, like Hora's, are not plagued by thorny issues of power, authority, and dependency. Only human hierarchies evoke those emotional and social troubles, the kinds that constantly plague organizations' managers. But suppose Hora's shop had grown into a ten- or twenty-person organization. Wouldn't he have used the same kind of thinking to arrange them into a human hierarchy? Then he would gain the pluses of mass production but also the new complexities that come with managing a human group.

Such hierarchical ways of thinking, in fact, tend to be the process of choice when we undertake all sorts of moderately complicated tasks. Outlining a chapter of this book is a hierarchical process. So is planning a vacation or building a house. Would any of us try to put together a model ship (or a real one) without a hierarchy? Wouldn't we, almost "naturally," begin with subassemblies—making the sails, putting the hull together, assembling the rudder, building a little lifeboat? Only then would we be likely to combine the subs into larger assemblies and then still larger ones. Would we do it differently if we were assembling automobiles? Maybe we can have small groups put together larger subunits in order to enrich jobs and increase productivity. But even within these groups there are doubtless hierarchical steps that must be taken. That hierarchical *process* is just common-sensible. We think hierarchy, but we don't think *about* hierarchy.

SIZE AND AGE DRIVE TOWARD HIERARCHY

You have surely noticed this book's repeated emphasis on hierarchies in *large* organizations. That's because not all organizations have to be predominantly and clearly hierarchical. Little start-ups can be put together in all sorts of ways, often in ways that are more productive and fulfilling than hierarchies. Like young people—and some old ones, too—young organizations can be highly flexible. They can operate without designated leaders or with widely shared leadership. They can modify themselves continually, as long as they (but not necessarily their occupants) remain young and small.

But if these small setups do good work, they survive, and if they survive they are almost certain to grow—more customers, more employees, more spacious facilities, more differentiated products and services. And they must perforce grow older. These two—growth and age—are something like a reverse magician. They turn little, egalitarian, silk-purse organizations into big sow's-ear hierarchies, and they do it without so much as a by-your-leave from the humans who inhabit them.

Over time, and with increasing size, hierarchy is sure to crash the party. Tighter controls sneak up on loose, open, everybody-contributes-to-everything little groups. Specialized roles and regular routines evolve, along with differentiation of authority, rank, rewards, status, and all the rest of hierarchy's standard accessories.

Growth, especially, drives organizations toward hierarchy. Why? It's because increased size is likely to be accompanied by increased complexity, and hierarchies are excellent mechanisms for coping with complexity. They don't control *all* complexity, but hierarchies help keep the whole expanding collection of people and tasks in a reasonably orderly state.

Even if they don't grow in size, just getting older almost always causes even the most rambunctious little outfits to "get organized." Over time, small, egalitarian organizations tend to become unstable. Issues of fairness arise. Interpersonal conflicts erupt. Certain tasks are routinized—payrolls, mail deliveries, tax records, files. So even small organizations, after they get their feet on the ground, find themselves setting up a few layers of hierarchy. They don't do it because some members want to seize power, although that can happen. They do it simply because it's a parsimonious way of coping with tensions and of effectively using people's energies. To avoid hierarchy, that is, small organizations must perform two rather difficult tricks: They must stay small, and they must stay young.

HIERARCHY IN, HUMANISM OUT?

Unfortunately, as hierarchy creeps into young organizations, passion and enthusiasm often creep out. As routine builds, excitement fades. And with hierarchy come the very kinds of psychological and social problems discussed earlier: distrust, distorted communication, territoriality, interpersonal and intergroup conflicts, and the others. Obviously, such problems can then vitiate many of hierarchies' projected advantages. For even though hierarchies may help us cope with complicated tasks, they also dehumanize us. They tend to impersonalize and formalize organizations, and resistance often follows.

Here's a broad, common-sense hypothesis about the relationship between organizational size and organizational humanism. Call it the "hierarchy in, humanism out" hypothesis: Larger organizations tend to be more hierarchical and hence more impersonal and rule-governed than smaller ones. So larger organizations should, other things being equal, be less humanistic than smaller ones.

I tried a quick and dirty test of that hypothesis this morning. I used the January 2003 issue of *Fortune* magazine's annual list of the

"100 Best Companies to Work For" as my database.[14] It was a sharply restricted distribution, but I figured smaller companies should rank closer to the top of that list than larger ones, even among that elite set. My rationale: Smaller companies were likely to be more "human," and more human companies were likely to be voted better places to work.

The results came out right (i.e., the way I wanted them to): The top 10 of those 100 best-companies-to-work-for averaged 7,802 employees, and the bottom 10 (ranks 91 through 100) averaged 15,642. But because one or two very large numbers could easily distort these figures, I checked the medians, the middle scores. The results were even better! Among the 10 best companies to work for, the median number of employees was 2,472. Among the bottom 10, the median number was 11,631.

Soon the January 2004 issue of *Fortune* arrived, so I replicated my "experiment" and got even clearer results. Among the top 10 of the 2004 list, the median for U.S. employees (*Fortune*'s 2004 ranking listed overseas employees separately) was 2,203. For the bottom 10 the median number was 20,243. If there were such a thing as a list of the 100 *worst* companies, would the median number of employees in the bottom 10 be humongous?

Of course, there were some very large enterprises among both the 2003 and the 2004 lists of 100 best. The number 1 company in 2003, for example, was no dwarf. It was Edward Jones, with 25,278 employees. FedEx, the largest of the 100 best with 172,569 people, ranked 72nd. In 2004, the number 1 company was J. M. Smucker, with 2,585 U.S. employees. But IBM (72nd, with 140,859 U.S. employees) and FedEx (96th, with 175,592 U.S. employees) also made the top 100. So, even big companies can make the list of best places to work.

Perhaps smaller outfits tend to be voted better places to work because in smaller units people are more likely to be real, recognizable people, with unique personalities, names, and faces. That's why Hewlett-Packard (which, curiously, did not make *Fortune*'s top 100 in either year, although it had been ranked 10 in both 1998 and 1999) used to try to keep itself small, even as it grew large. If any unit grew to more than 1,500 employees, it was split. Now, big companies are trying all sorts of other devices to help them act small even though they are very large. They're doing that in an effort to pick up some of the speed and vitality that are characteristic of smaller, more human organizations, without giving up the enormous economic advantages of large size.

The Paradox of Governance by Impersonal Laws

There is a partial paradox here: In nation-states, when the rule of law replaces the rule of a single, all-powerful sovereign, we are likely to view that change as a great leap forward, away from autocracy, toward democracy. That's what the brand new United States of America dared to try for the first time in modern history, and we applaud it still.

In small, egalitarian, but growing organizations, however, the arrival of an equivalent to the rule of law, the rule of policies, can push us the other way. Even when the policies are mutually agreed upon, they can displace a more or less informal, perhaps more egalitarian form of shared governance. Such formalization can move the group toward impersonal, arm's-length relationships and can place increasing limitations on individual autonomy.

At first we may view such changes as positive, because they free us from chaotic disorder. Later, however, we may reverse course, viewing the same changes as restrictive. Now we must obtain three signatures and write formal requests before we can take even simple actions. Such "policies" may initially enter organizations for positive reasons, in the interest of distributive justice and productivity, but more regulated work environments also drain freedom and humanism.

Would we, or could we, have it any other way? A village may be able to manage with a part-time mayor and a single part-time policeman, but should New York or London abandon its governmental structure so that its citizens can have more personal space? Might that not stimulate a bit too much creativity? Do we really want our big organizations to be governed entirely informally? Wouldn't that sharply increase our vulnerability to emergent autocracy? We need rules in organizations. Many of the ones that frustrate us by restricting our freedom actually help, in a larger sense, to protect it.

THE WORLD IS WATCHING US

Why do hierarchies persist? In part, it's because there's a world out there, beyond the institutional gate. Our larger environments are not just sleeping dogs, lying inert and irrelevant. There are packs of snarling pit bulls out there, growling at organizations, pressuring them, demanding that they live by their societies' codes and rules. There are land mines out there. Governmental controls lie in wait for innocent trespassers. There are scary financial markets, predatory takeover artists, and all sorts of pressure groups. There are competitors, too, old familiar ones and unforeseen new ones that suddenly pop up out of nowhere. And there is a continuous inflow of innovations, technological and managerial, that every organization must ingest if it is to keep abreast of its markets.

Such forces keep tweaking organizations. Even if a small company could hie itself off to a deserted island, sooner or later it would have to relate to those worldly pressures. Trying to do so will surely drive growing organizations toward hierarchy, toward internal control systems that tie down loose cannons and inadvertently tie down everything else as well.

IN SUMMARY

This chapter discusses why hierarchies go on and on. It has offered both psychological and pragmatic reasons for hierarchies' long-standing and continuing viability. Human hierarchies, for example, are psychological magnets that attract achievement-driven men and women. They reward us with more than just the money to pay our rent. They give us opportunities to achieve power, status, and wealth, to climb our vaunted ladders to success. They give us social identity cards to help us maintain the illusion that we are both significant and secure in an insecure world. Although we complain about the negatives of life behind hierarchies' walls—about boring routines, toxic bosses, and the rest—we also collude with those hierarchies to get our share of the goodies they dangle before us. Their requirements of conformity and obedience are almost ideally suited to our ethic of individual achievement.

Hierarchies also hang on for different, more pragmatic reasons, largely independent of their human occupants. For example, hierarchies are great devices for coping with complexity. They make organizational sense for some of the same reasons that they make sense for individuals when we take on complicated tasks. Growth and age also drive organizations toward hierarchies. As organizations grow, hierarchy helps them simplify things. And as organizations age, they set up hierarchical routines to keep costs down and orderliness up.

For such reasons, then, and others, hierarchies are likely to stay with us. And they will continue to need a clan of middle managers to keep them going. We complain about hierarchies, disparage them, and try to convince ourselves that they are finished. But they are not finished. They will go on because they protect and reward us and allow us to achieve. And they will go on because they help us get big jobs done. They will repopulate themselves, too, as new organizations grow. And they will continue for other reasons, well beyond the purview of this book, reasons to be found in such diverse realms as economics and biology.

It's time now to move beyond the question of why hierarchies just keep going. We shall look at how big organizational hierarchies have evolved and changed and at how those changes have affected the lives and work of middle managers. That's what part II is about.

PART II

HIERARCHIES AND ORGANIZATIONAL CHANGE

*P*art I of this book asked why *questions: Why do organizational hierarchies, with all their flaws, just keep going? Part II is about how questions: How do hierarchies manage to stay alive despite the stormy social and technological changes that keep reshaping their worlds? How do they cope with the humanizing attacks that have for decades been mounted against them? How have they themselves changed? And how do those organizations' middle managers cope with the mixed bag of changes that their organizations expect them to integrate?*

Chapter 3 is about systemizing and humanizing, two different ways of thinking about organizations. These two concepts have been changing and counter-changing big organizations for at least a hundred years. The tensions between them have not torn organizational hierarchies apart but rather have actually helped them adapt to their changing environments. And they have also kept middle managers hopping.

Chapter 4 looks at three major changes—each stimulated by the ongoing humanizing–systemizing tensions—that have helped hierarchical organizations prosper but have also generated complicating problems of their own. Chapter 5 considers how big hierarchies manage to ingest all sorts of changes and innovations and yet maintain their basic structural form.

THREE

Humanizing Hierarchies Versus Systemizing Them

For decades, indeed centuries, an ideological war has been quietly raging in and around organizations. It has been mostly a cold war, although more than once it has gotten hot, even physical. The war has been between two major combatants, two streams of thought; call them the *humanizing* stream and the *systemizing* stream. The two may not be quite as polarized as I am caricaturing them here, but most of the differences are sharp and real. Over the years, of course, the warring sides have shifted and changed, forming new alliances and developing new weapons. Sometimes members of one army have deserted to the other. Sometimes peripheral members of each side have gotten together in search of peaceful cease-fires. The two underlying ideologies, though, are still mostly the same, and the battle goes on.

A HUNDRED YEARS OF TENSION

Humanizing and systemizing are two opposing belief systems, two *weltanshauungs;* two visions of how organizations should be designed and managed. It is through one or the other of these ideological lenses and often through both—one lens with one eye and its opposite with the other—that organizations assess their changing environments and decide how to deal with this new technology or that social upheaval.

Organizations for People, or People for Organizations?

The sharpest and most intransigent difference between humanizers and systemizers can perhaps be characterized this way: The humanizing stream treats humans as masters, and organizations as instruments in humans' service. In contrast, the systemizing stream treats organizations as masters, and humans as one of many resources in organizations' service. That such opposites should coexist within the same large organization is illogical, but the fact is that large organizations are roomy enough to accommodate many such inconsistencies, and for long periods. Perhaps that's because much of the time the humanizing and systemizing perspectives travel in parallel, with neither paying much attention to the other.

Periodically, however, the two ways of thinking collide. When that happens, turbulence ensues, with the systemizing view almost always driving the organization toward more hierarchy and the humanizing view driving toward less. And where are those collisions most likely to occur? As we shall see in part III, they occur mostly at the places where middle managers are trying to do their jobs.

These two kinds of thinking don't coexist only "out there," in organizations. They also coexist inside our individual heads. For example, I consider myself a true-blue, card-carrying humanizer. Yet the cognitive good sense of the systemizing perspective sneaks through often enough to make me cast an occasional crossover vote for its side, even against the socioemotional good sense of my humanizing side. It's hard to reject all of what either humanizers or systemizers are fighting for.

Here are some other characteristics of each of the two streams:

- Humanizers are sensitive to soft realities: trust, emotion, relationships, empathy, and imagination. They think and talk about such things all the time. Operationally, these concerns translate into human relations programs, team-building activities, motivational seminars, sensitivity training, and organizational development departments. The first-order intents of all these is to enhance personal growth, improve morale, intensify motivation, encourage creativity, and increase collaboration. The second-order intent is to increase organizations' productivity and flexibility.

Systemizers, in contrast, focus on hard realities: on logic, consistency, effectiveness, discipline. They go in for words such as *rigor, facts,* and *the bottom line.* Operationally, this perspective translates into financial and other control systems, improved measurement and planning methods, and clear specifications of lines of authority and responsibility. The broad intent of these constructs is to make organizations as efficient, responsive, and productive as possible.

- The humanizing view, eager to maximize human effectiveness, prefers rather untamed organizational gardens. They want to raise a wide range of human flora that bloom in a profusion of sizes and colors, each according to its nature— flowers for all seasons. They want to fertilize their garden with TLC so that each of its occupants can become whatever it is able to become.

   Systemizers, seeking to maximize organizations' effectiveness, prefer orderly, Japanese-style gardens, each plant carefully placed, each tree precisely pruned, trained, wired, and shaped. They want to sculpt and pare humans' behavior to fit their organizational designs.

- The humanizers' major organizational thrust has thus been toward joy, personal fulfillment, and productivity via loosely organized or non-hierarchical structures. Humanizers want to free up organizations' members to release their presumably enormous untapped intellectual and creative potential, thereby providing meaning to people's lives and effectiveness to their organizations.

   Systemizers go the other way. They see humans as one of an organization's several types of relevant resources. Systemizers prefer to control, adumbrate, and regulate people's behavior, to do with people what they would do with any other pieces of equipment: shape them and fine-tune them for the specific jobs that need to be done.

- Humanizers celebrate human diversity, because diversity, they feel, is one route to organizational nirvana. It is via diverse individuals and groups that creativity and other, not always well-specified, good things can be maximized.

   Systemizers don't cotton to the randomness and variability that accompany diversity. They see diversity—*not* diversity in race or gender, but diversity in the ways people do their work—as an obstacle to the achievement of good order. We humans come in too wide a variety of shapes and sizes for systemizers, so they want to make us more uniform, to minimize random variations among people, just as they would minimize random variations in other raw materials or equipment. Indeed, at the extreme, systemizers would just as soon get rid of people altogether, if they could find a more standardized, reliable alternative.

- Humanizers talk constantly about *leadership.*
   Systemizers talk about *management.*

- Humanizers always seem to have a few special, favorite companies that exemplify their humanizing perspective. Perhaps that's because humanizers tend to view themselves as organizational outsiders, a minority not fully accepted by the massive systemizing establishment. In the 1950s and 1960s it was mostly small companies that made humanizers' A-list: Dewey and Almy Chemical Co. (later absorbed by W.R. Grace), along with Dr. Alfred Marrow's very participative Harwood Manufacturing Co. and small companies seeking union-management cooperation via the then-new Scanlon Plan.[1] In the 1970s, Saga Foods and HP, along with Sweden's Volvo, had become favorites. By the 1980s, it was Herman Miller, the furniture manufacturer, and several Japanese companies. Then, in the 1990s, more networked organizations like Swiss/Swedish ABB and group-oriented companies like Hewlett-Packard were among the chosen. It's not yet clear, at least to me, which companies will emerge as the humanizing favorites of the new millennium. My guess is that they will be large, not small, companies and that the emphasis will continue to be on innovative, humanizing modifications of mostly systemizing hierarchies.

Systemizers' special favorites have been large companies, such as Ford Motor Company in the 1950s, Litton Industries, ITT, and TRW in the 1960s and 1970s. Later, in the 1990s, GE, Wal-Mart, and, for a while, Enron, with its "creative" new business model, were in the systemizers' spotlight. And perhaps we should add the late Arthur Andersen, the company that was often called, because of its renowned internal discipline, the "Marine Corps" of accounting firms.

The continuing conflict between humanizers and systemizers has taken many forms. Sometimes, the two have engaged in small skirmishes inside a particular organization's walls. Occasionally, however, the clash broadens, as each side's intellectual, political, social, and even quasi-military allies enter the fray. And of course, both humanizers and systemizers have steadily modernized their weaponry. Like other long wars, this one has become increasingly sophisticated and potentially more lethal.

Most of the time, systemizers have controlled the high ground and the major hierarchical citadels. It is the systemizers who keep rebuilding and reinforcing hierarchies, while humanizers snipe at them and bombard them from outside and below. Occasionally humanizers win battles, but neither side ever definitively wins the war. Occasionally, too, peace talks occur, valiant efforts to resolve the major differences between the two sides.

The Struggle Goes On

Despite all attempts to end their long battle, the tensions between these two worldviews—humanizing and systemizing—keep recurring. Sometimes the conflict is clothed as an issue of governance, sometimes as a labor relations issue, or, especially in universities, as a duel between the hard-headed (or wannabe hard-headed) disciplines and soft-headed, not-quite disciplines. The battle in academia can occur even within single departments. That happened, for example, between the physiological psychologists and the clinical and social psychologists at Harvard many years ago. It also happened between the quantitative and not-so-quantitative sociologists at Chicago and later within the finance group at the Stanford Business School.

This ongoing yin/yang dispute has produced positive as well as negative effects. It has caused great hierarchies to change, to modernize, sometimes to tighten up and sometimes to loosen, sometimes to become more authoritarian and sometimes less.

Humanizers occasionally think "unrealistically," with some of them asserting, as an earlier chapter pointed out, that they've won the war or that they've killed off hierarchies or at least have made them turn tail. But systemizers, who pride themselves on their rationality, also occasionally think in dangerously lopsided, hyperrational ways. In mid-2003, for example, the U.S. Department of Defense rolled out a systemizing plan to establish "an online futures trading market where speculators could bet on the probabilities of terrorist attacks, assassinations and coups."[2] The systemizers who put this idea together had empirical data showing that multiple judgments about future events, each backed with cash on the line, would collectively turn out to be somewhat more accurate than most other varieties of forecasts. That perfectly rational notion—that "markets are extremely efficient, effective and timely aggregators of dispersed and even hidden information . . . often better than expert opinions"[3]—was greeted with a firestorm of "emotional," humanizing noise. The idea was shouted down as immoral, stupid, "so insane it must have been a hoax."

The uprising against the futures market notion must surely have helped confirm many systemizers' opinion that most people simply don't think straight. If they were more coolly logical, they wouldn't reject such a perfectly sensible idea for such hotheaded non-reasons. Indeed, a week or so after the plan was withdrawn, an op-ed piece in the *Wall Street Journal* came to its belated defense in a typically hyperrational, emotion-free, systemizing way: "Such markets would price risks visibly and more efficiently than they do today. The effect would be not only a better allocation of capital but valuable culling of information that is difficult to assemble otherwise."[4]

No humanizing element in that systemizing equation!

A BIT OF HISTORY: THE ENDLESS DIVIDE

In 1950, Dr. Temple Burling, a humanizing industrial psychiatrist at Cornell University, wrote an essay with a title that continues to stick in my mind. He called it "You Can't Hire a Hand."[5] It was common-place back then to talk about companies "hiring hands," as in "farm hands." Like it or not, Burling pointed out, you can't hire a hand without all the other human attachments bundled in: brains, hearts, values, beliefs, and a sundry collection of other heavy baggage.

Over the decades, indeed over the centuries, systemizing-dominated organizations have tried to hire hands. They were also ready to abandon those hands in favor of cheaper, more reliable alternatives whenever such alternatives, usually newly invented machines, became available. However, the accompaniments to those hands—hearts, brains, and feelings—didn't usually like the hand-hiring idea to begin with, and they disliked even more the idea of having their hands replaced by machines. So again and again, the whole human being has fought back.

Almost two hundred years ago, for example, in Nottingham, England, General Ned Ludd's Luddites got so fired up about labor-saving new frames being installed in local textile mills that they raided several mills and trashed the frames. Things got so bad that Parliament passed "The Frame Breaking Act"—despite the impassioned protests of sympathetic humanizers such as Lord Byron—making such destruction a capital offense. In April 1812, seventeen Luddites were hanged. Even today, one can put down people who question some technological innovation on humanistic grounds by labeling them "Luddites."

That theme—heroic figures (or anarchistic ones, depending on which side you're on) resisting the incursion of heartless machines—recurs throughout industrial history. Remember the folk ballad about John Henry's battle with the steam drill? That legend is based on the blasting of the Big Bend Tunnel, more than a mile long, straight through a solid rock mountain in West Virginia. Steel-drivin' men like John Henry used ten-pound hammers to drive steel rods into the rock—until tunnel engineers tried to replace the men with steam-driven drills. John Henry challenged the steam drill to a steel-driving contest. This is a classic verse from one of the many folk ballads that ensued:

> *John Henry said to his captain,*
> *"A man, he ain't nothin' but a man.*
> *And before I'd let your steam drill beat me down,*
> *I'd die with the hammer in my hand, Lord, Lord!*
> *I'd die with the hammer in my hand."*[6]

John Henry won the battle but died of the effort, a martyr to the human spirit. And although his larger-than-life statue still stands at the entrance to the Big Bend Tunnel, steel-drivin' men have long since been replaced by more productive, less troublesome systemizing technologies.

Four decades after John Henry, the humanizing and systemizing streams again clashed when Henry Ford invented his enormously productive, systemizing assembly line. Humanizers fought back with weapons ranging from strikes and labor unions to Charlie Chaplin's great humanizing film *Modern Times,* a dark caricature of the human costs of work on the line. But strikes and other protests notwithstanding, the assembly line won that battle.

At about the same time, Frederick Winslow Taylor, engineer extraordinaire, introduced a systemizing work measurement method he called Scientific Management, a method that stirred the wrath of humanizers everywhere. Here, for example, are short excerpts from an exchange of letters-to-the-editor that appeared in the *American Magazine* in 1911, just about a century after the Luddites.[7] Taylor had written an article extolling the virtues of his new Scientific Management. Upton Sinclair (a then famous, partially humanizing do-gooder, author of what many consider the first American best-seller, *The Jungle,* and once a Socialist candidate for governor of California) took umbrage at Taylor's article. He wrote this irate response:

> *He [Mr. Taylor] tells us how workingmen were loading twelve and*
> *a half tons of pig iron and he induced them to load forty-seven*
> *tons instead. They had formerly been getting $1.15; he paid them*
> *$1.85. . . . I shall not soon forget the picture that he gave us of the*

poor old laborer who was trying to build his pitiful little home after hours, and who was induced to give 362 per cent. more service for 61 per cent. more pay. . . .

I, as you may perhaps know, am one of those Utopian persons who do not believe that the working class of America will forever consent to produce $1,000 worth of value and get $168 in return. I believe that the time will come when they will take possession of the instruments and means of production. . . .[8]

Rational, fact-oriented, precise, systemizing Taylor then replied. Here are excerpts:

Doubtless some of those . . . like Mr. Upton Sinclair will complain because under Scientific Management the workman when he is shown how to do twice as much work as he formerly did is not paid twice his former wages . . . [But] as we have before stated, the pig-iron handler is not an extraordinary man difficult to find; he is merely a man more or less of the type of the ox, heavy both mentally and physically. . . .

[Further,] a long series of experiments . . . has demonstrated the fact that when workmen of the caliber of the pig-iron handler . . . are paid wages up to 60 per cent. beyond the wages usually paid . . . this increase in wages tends to make them not only more thrifty but better men in every way; that they live rather better, begin to save money, become more sober, and work more steadily. When . . . they receive much more than 60 per cent. increase in wages, many of them will work irregularly and tend to become more or less shiftless, extravagant and dissipated.[9]

Note how easily the humanizing–systemizing conflict can metamorphose from a discussion about one laborer's work into generalizations about the nature of human nature and grand issues of public policy. Sinclair uses Taylor's views as an argument for that quaint old socialist dogma about taking possession of the means of production, and Taylor prefers to wrap his view of the pig-iron handler (Taylor called him Schmitt) in the systemizing aura of science and empiricism (e.g., "A long series of experiments . . . has demonstrated the *fact*" that people like Schmitt will just get drunk if they get paid too much).

(An aside here, and not an apologetic one: If I seem a bit strident about all this, I ask your forbearance. But even today, Taylor's characterization of those early twentieth-century immigrants as shiftless, dissipated "oxen" gets my dander up. He's talking about my father and many of your grandfathers and great grandfathers. Taylor's oxen were our heroes, men and women who had the guts and skill to make their way to America in search of the good life for their children and their children's children. Their get-up-and-go would have made Abe Lincoln proud.)

Innovations like Ford's assembly line and Taylor's Scientific Management reinforced the hierarchy by sharpening the separation between the organizational planning and implementing phases of the whole managing process. Before Taylor, for example, each pig-iron handler made his own decisions about how to pace himself, how to hoist iron, and how to pile it. These were tiny decisions, perhaps, but each worker made them, using his head as well as his hands. After Taylor, an industrial engineer, stopwatch in hand, made even those minuscule decisions, leaving only the doing part to Mr. Schmitt. Clearly that was, at least in the short term, a more efficient way to operate. But what systemizing Taylorists saw as "efficiency," the Schmitts of the world and their intellectual and political supporters saw as involuntary psychological brain surgery. For what can extirpate anyone's humanity more than the revocation of the right to think for oneself? Taylor, incidentally, was thus establishing a convenient self-fulfilling prophecy. By first decorticating him, he was guaranteeing that Schmitt would indeed act "the type of the ox."

THE 1950S: HUMANIZERS FIGHT BACK

Taylor's Scientific Management wasn't the end of the battle between humanizing and systemizing. In the 1950s, the anti-hierarchy humanizers and the pro-hierarchy systemizers clashed again. This time the humanizers didn't exactly win, but they captured a good deal of terrain.

One tiny skirmish of that great battle took place at MIT, where a handful of us were graduate students. We were proud and perhaps arrogant acolytes of Doug McGregor, the pioneering humanizer of Theory Y fame. Our hot little group called itself "the people-people" and inhabited the third floor of MIT's Building 1. Our systemizing enemy—the hard-headed accounting, finance, and "principles of management" people, along with Taylor's progeny, the industrial engineers—held down the first floor of the same building.

We people-people were sometimes required to take first-floor courses, all sorts of systemizing foolishness about such inhuman stuff as financial controls and cost accounting. As you might guess, those forays into enemy territory served only to shore up our faith in our third floor's humanizing creed. And as our commitment to that creed grew, so did our scorn for the first floor's apostasy. Those first-floor guys were blind to Truth down there, intransigent, prejudiced, just plain wrong. They had adding machines where their hearts should have been. They didn't even comprehend our sacred words: *morale, motivation, participation.* We called the first-floor folks "make-a-buck Neanderthals." They called us "the happiness boys."

That surprisingly productive conflict was not limited to MIT. Similar battles were erupting in business organizations, in the military, and in universities everywhere. We humanizers were hot in the 1950s, certain that our cause was right and righteous. We were designing a gloriously democratic, egalitarian organizational future. It was a heady time, a time when participative management made a good-sized dent in the hard, systemizing armor of large hierarchies.

The Rise of Information Technology

The rest of the world, however, wasn't standing still. By the 1960s the information age had begun. Early forms of information technology were causing the systemizing stream to widen into a great river. Organizations seized upon IT's newly invented, low-energy control machines to tighten their hierarchies and to replace some simple forms of human decision making. That was when words such as *cybernetics, automation, artificial intelligence,* and *robotization* began to enter our lexicons. Old systemizing technologies, including

Scientific Management's time study, were phasing out. Quantitative analyses were phasing in. Departments of Operations Research and Management Science were being formed in businesses and business schools. These information-related technologies were putting systemizers back into hierarchies' catbird seats.

At that point, some of us (including me) wrongly forecast the demise of the middle manager.[10] If computers could quickly process huge quantities of information, we reasoned, decision making would become more centralized. Large hierarchies, à la Alfred P. Sloan's General Motors, had recently been decentralizing. But, we argued, they weren't decentralizing because they had seen the humanizing light. Rather, they were decentralizing because they were being forced to do so. They had become so big, and their environments so volatile, that lower ranks, closer to the action, had to be granted more autonomy to make decisions.

Now, however, with the arrival of high-speed computers, top management would be able to get all the information it needed in real time. So the top could now do what it had always wanted to do. It could *really* centralize. It could run even huge multi-ringed organizational circuses right from the CEO's office. We were predicting (but not recommending) flattened hierarchies (like Drucker's "orchestral" organizations) for exactly the opposite reasons that such flattening is currently being touted. Today's humanizers want to flatten in order to devolve power away from the top, to distribute authority more widely. We expected flattening because power could and would now be more concentrated at the top. Hierarchies wouldn't need all those intervening middle managers.

Our forecast didn't quite pan out—or did it? We hadn't counted on the miniaturization and mass production of the PC, nor the consequent wide dissemination of real-time information throughout the organization. Nor had we counted on huge increases in the size and complexity of organizational tasks. IT changed many middle-level jobs and displaced many others. Middle managers, however, certainly did not disappear. But is power now truly *less* concentrated at the tops of large hierarchies? Are employees of large organizations really freer, more autonomous now? Or has ever-more sophisticated information technology—despite the inroads of participative management—invented new tools to replicate century-old Ford- and Taylor-type top-down methods, this time among service and other white-collar workers and middle managers, too?[11]

A Systemizing Future?

One branch of the systemizing stream's possible future direction looks quite clear. A new breed of systemizers (many of them would doubtless object to that label) is building machines that can think, imagine, move, decide, and do pretty much anything people can do—only better. Thus, an IT insider, Bill Joy, former chief scientist at Sun Microsystems, in a much-cited article, asserts that such machines will soon be with us.[12] And in a 1999 book, *The Age of Spiritual Machines*, Ray Kurzweil (who holds *nine* honorary degrees) makes a similar forecast.[13] Joy and Kurzweil may be overly optimistic, but just as it was imprudent for many of us to deny the managerial relevance of early computers (IBM's Thomas Watson predicted, in 1943, that "there is a world market for about five computers"[14]), it seems equally imprudent for the rest of us to ignore their informed judgments.

Let's also consider the most likely secondary effects of such machines on the never-ending intra-hierarchical battle between humanizers and systemizers. How about this, for example: When and if machines really do replace most humans—with middle managers near the top of the list of the expendables—will the humanizing–systemizing relationship have come full circle? With few humans left on the organizational stage, humanizers will have little to complain about. Human issues of motivation, authoritarianism, and the rest will have become irrelevant, but perhaps only for a while. Market forces should lead to the eventual recall of at least some idled humans, who would be available at bargain prices, to do menial tasks unworthy of expensive machines. Then people might again become the pig-iron handling oxen of those organizations, now reporting up the hierarchy to boss machines. Perhaps then a brave bottom-rung John Henry machine, threatened with displacement by a cheaper human, will try to prove its own spiritual worth. Will the humanizing–systemizing battle then begin all over again? If that happens, Henry David Thoreau's comment, made in another context, will again ring true: "But lo! Men have become the tools of their tools."

Even if such machines do successfully drive humans out of organizational hierarchies, will they also kill off the hierarchy itself? That seems unlikely. Hierarchies are too abundant and omnipresent in complex man–machine systems, as well as in nature's things and creatures. They made sense for Hora, the watchmaker. The Microsoft dictionary says that they also make sense for building computer hardware and software:

> Hierarchies are characteristic of several aspects of computing because they provide organizational frameworks that can reflect logical links, or relationships, between separate records, files, or pieces of equipment. For example, hierarchies are used in organizing related files on a disk, related records in a database, and related (interconnected) devices on a network. In applications such as spreadsheets, hierarchies of a sort are used to establish the order of precedence in which arithmetic operations are to be performed by the computer.[15]

Hierarchies even make sense for our human bodies. They, too, are made up of hierarchically arranged systems—skeletal, digestive, circulatory, nervous, and many other systems—each comprising several subsystems, and each of those having sub-subsystems of its own. Such hierarchies should make as much sense in people-less systems as they do everywhere else.

SYSTEMIZING IS HUMAN, TOO

Let's not leave this chapter without making sure that we set one thing straight. Whatever the future of hierarchies' simultaneous humanizing and systemizing, we humanizers should quit advertising ourselves as sole protectors of the human spirit and setting up systemizers as black-hatted control freaks. The systemizing vision is different from the humanizing one, but it is also an indisputably human vision. Isn't even the most dedicated humanizer among us also something of a systemizer? Systemizing belongs as naturally to every one of us as curiosity itself, as naturally as our deep drive to bring order out of chaos, to program what has hitherto lain unprogrammed. Indeed most of us seem to love to systemize almost as much as we love to humanize. We—including managers—love to solve puzzles, to figure things out, to bring order to our worlds.

Sure, we feel good when we're fat and well fed, but sometimes we feel even better when we're lean and hungry—hungry to make things happen, to explore the unknown, to solve the unsolved problem. Some of systemizing, that is, also goes by more attractive aliases—including some that humanizers usually claim as theirs alone—such as trying, creating, exploring, innovating, and just working. It's our restless systemizing side that invents and manufactures the CDs, builds the BMWs, pushes us to reach for the stars, and makes us construct the huge hierarchies that will eventually take us there.

IN SUMMARY

For convenience, this chapter has divided much organizational "theory" into two ways of envisioning human organizations: humanizing and systemizing. The two have been presented as though they were polar opposites, something that in reality is not quite the case. Humanizers focus on the people side of organizations, on human needs, attitudes, and emotions. They are generally opposed to hierarchies, viewing them as restrictive, spirit-draining, even imprisoning. Systemizers, in contrast, fixate on facts, measurements, and systems. They are generally in favor of hierarchies, treating them as effective structures for doing big jobs. Humanizers tend to stereotype systemizers as insensitive, anal-retentive types who think that if they can't measure it, it isn't there. Systemizers tend to caricature humanizers as fuzzy-headed, overemotional creatures who don't think straight.

Humanizers' efforts to defang or eliminate hierarchies is as old as the struggle for the rights of individuals. The humanizers' position runs something like this: Hierarchies are carrot-and-stick instruments. They have always been exploited by tyrants to control and delude their subjects. They infantilize us humans. And although most modern industrial hierarchies are not the absolutist regimes of old, they still necessarily restrict our freedom, thereby pressing us into childlike dependency.

Systemizers counter that we need hierarchical organizations to get the world's work done, to govern societies, to produce goods and services, and generally to maintain our thin layer of civilization. We humans must pay some behavioral bills to win such good things.

In and around organizations, humanizers and systemizers are battling still, but no longer with spears and arrows. Both are now equipped with more deadly high-tech weaponry. Because large organizations are cognitively very spacious, both have been successful in influencing large hierarchies to change, often in near contradictory ways. Chapter 4 considers three of those changes and explores how they have affected large organizations and the managers who work within them.

FOUR

Three Changes That Shook the Hierarchy

Today's hierarchies certainly aren't your daddy's hierarchies. They've changed. They've been pushed and pulled by humanizers and systemizers, and they've been pressured by swirling technological and social gales. Nor have they all been alike. Some have shrunk, succumbed, or been cannibalized, whereas others have prospered by adapting, innovating, or doing the cannibalizing. They're still changing, but they're still hierarchies.

This chapter describes three important ways in which many big organizational hierarchies have changed. These changes have sometimes simultaneously loosened and tightened, flattened and steepened them, making them more livable in some ways and more imprisoning in others. Moreover, these changes also have had major effects on the working lives of organizations' managers.

Humanizing forces drove the first of the three changes, *participative management* (PM). Systemizers' exploitation of emerging new technologies, especially information technology, propelled the second, *analytic management* (AM). The third change—unforeseen, and, once seen, actively disinvited—has been the emergence of a *hot groups* style of management. Hot groups can best be characterized as a mixed breed. They were neither the product of humanizing nor of systemizing thought. They have some features of both, but most of their characteristics are uniquely their own.

What follows is a fuller explication of each of the three and some of their effects on hierarchies and managers.

PARTICIPATIVE MANAGEMENT: HUMANIZING HIERARCHIES

In the 1950s, shortly after World War II, participative management (initially called "human relations") made a serious move into American organizations. It moved in, with considerable difficulty, on what was at that time a generally top-down, authoritarian managerial style, a way of managing that tended to view people as one of several classic economic "factors of production."

The humanizing ideas underlying PM had been around for a long time. Mary Parker Follett persuasively made the people-first case back in the 1920s, and so did Harvard's Elton Mayo and Fritz Roethlisberger.[1] Later, just after the war, a small set of influential American academics—among them Douglas McGregor at MIT, Rensis Likert at Michigan, Abraham Maslow then at Brooklyn College, and Peter Drucker then at NYU—began a concerted drive toward what Norbert Wiener later called "the human use of human beings."[2] They wanted to build a truly new way of managing, a way that was both humane and productive and that was appropriate to the expansive new postwar era. They wanted humanistic Theory Y to replace cynical old, people-are-inherently-lazy Theory X; industrial democracy to supplant autocracy; participation in lieu of top-down command and control; and management by objective instead of management by fiat; and they even wanted a new emphasis on the importance of small, collaborative groups. Moreover, this rapidly growing group was busily inventing actionable methods and techniques that would bring its ideas to life: survey methods, group development methods, counseling methods, experiential learning methods, and more. By the late 1950s Americans were not alone in these developments. Other innovative, largely humanizing concepts and methods were being built in the United Kingdom, the Netherlands, France, and Scandinavia.

These humanizing ideas got their big chance in the 1950s because organizations and much of the world were in a postwar "unfrozen" state. It was an upbeat, optimistic time. Expectations ran high. Old social barriers were weakening. Women had entered the work force in large numbers during World War II, and although many dropped out when the war ended, many others would never quit the labor force.[3] *All* employees now expected to be treated with respect. It was also a time to shake up old-fashioned business schools. All in all, the 1950s was a decade of organizational, managerial, and educational renewal, a time when even radical new participative ideas were able to squeeze through the company gate.

Participative Management Gets into Trouble

In most U.S. companies, the initial impact of participative management was not what its champions had intended. PM was aimed mostly at blue-collar workers, in part because shop floor workers were then the most numerous group of employees in large hierarchies, and most had been "Taylorized." Down there at that first level, however, PM got caught in a pincers movement. On one side—from the right—old-style "do-it-my-way" supervisors didn't take to goody-goody participative notions. They worried about losing (you may remember this old phrase) their "managerial prerogatives." Nor did traditional business schools like PM. They correctly perceived it as a threat to their standard systemizing course outlines. So they joined the attack.

Much to the dismay of PM's proponents, many trade unionists also took up arms against PM. Why? Unions had been designed to fight hard-nosed, top-down hierarchy. It was an enemy they knew and understood. This new participative stuff might change all that. To many trade unionists, PM looked like just another management ploy, a sneaky attempt to woo workers away from their unions. Some national unions even rejected the participative Scanlon Plan though an outstanding union executive had designed it and many local unions supported it.[4]

All the way into the 1980s, PM continued to be viewed with some suspicion by both management and labor. Here's a minor example: Once, in the early 1980s, a crusty, savvy labor union veteran gave a guest lecture in my humanizing Organizational Behavior course in the Stanford Executive Program. "What those human relations boys have really done," he told the class, "is dress up supervisors in pink jumpsuits. Just underneath, they're still the same hard-assed tyrants they've always been." For the students, forty-year-old executives already uncomfortable with all this "charm school" stuff, this speech really resonated. For once they were on the same wavelength as a union guy. So, of course, the students forthwith presented their charm school professor with a ravishing pink twill jumpsuit.

Participative Management Escapes—Upward

Why didn't that three-pronged attack by old-time management, old-time business schools, and old-time labor succeed in killing off weak, young participative management? In part, it was because some social scientists, mostly European, tried, with considerable success, to promote an active armistice via what came to be called the "sociotechnical systems" approach, a methodology that sought to integrate participative management with work-floor engineering.[5]

For the most part, though, and especially in the United States, PM escaped the pincers by climbing a couple of rungs up the hierarchical ladder. Upstairs, on the fast-growing white-shirted floors, among the new knowledge workers and middle managers, the participative idea received a warmer reception. You couldn't just order around this new breed of knowledge workers and managers. These folks worked with their heads, not their hands. They weren't unionized, and neither did they respond well to whips. So PM turned out to be just the right style at the right time for the new, expanding waistlines of large hierarchies. Add to that business schools' realization that these knowledge types were a rapidly growing, lucrative new market for participative-style management development programs.

PM's initial impact thus turned out to be somewhat different from what its founders had intended. Instead of the new participative style loosening the hierarchy, it very often reinforced it. It did so by widening the gap separating downstairs blue-collar people, who continued to be managed mostly in old, authoritarian ways, from new, upstairs, white-collar knowledge workers, for whom humanistic PM became the managerial order of the day. That difference was something like the difference, in the military, between the treatment of enlisted men and that of officers. It increased the significance of hierarchical rank, differentiating, even more sharply than before, between "somebodies and nobodies."[6]

Unexpected Help from the East

In the late 1970s, participative management made a sudden, unexpected great leap forward. It circled all the way around via Japan, whose high productivity, low prices, and excellent product quality were scaring American manufacturers. To find out how the Japanese were doing it, Western academics and executives began to swarm all over Nippon. A spate of best-selling books was quick to provide the answers, among them William Ouchi's *Theory Z* and Pascale and Athos's *The Art of Japanese Management.*[7] One thing they discovered was that some Japanese "secrets" had made their way to Japan via an American, W. Edwards Deming. Much of the Japanese success, these books also told Western managers, was not the result of better systemizing technology but rather of better humanizing practices, wiser employment methods, Japanese-style teamwork, the concept of lifelong employment, and a high level of mutual loyalty between employees and their companies.

Reacting—and sometimes overreacting—remarkably quickly to competitive realities, big Western organizations, especially American manufacturers, hurried to reinforce their humanizing, participative sides, this time all the way down the hierarchy. They began adapting Japanese styles to American organizational cultures: self-managed teams, quality circles, new organizational development techniques, and sometimes morning calisthenics. All these changes modified the tough old hierarchy, loosening it here, softening it there, dressing more of its managers in pink jumpsuits.

Smart Western companies, moreover, noticed something else about their Japanese counterparts. They weren't just participative. They were also doing some new analytic *systemizing,* introducing methods such as just-in-time scheduling and total quality management. And that brings us to the second big change: the rise of analytic management.

ANALYTIC MANAGEMENT: MODERNIZING INFORMATION AND CONTROL SYSTEMS

In the United States, it was ex-Pentagon planners and quantitative academics who spearheaded this second major change, a sharp shift toward analytic management. Onto the 1960s stage marched this new, tough-minded, by-the-numbers, systemizing approach to the managing process. Its heroes were the unsmiling, fact-oriented industrialists of the 1960s: Roy Ash of Litton, Harold Geneen of ITT, and perhaps most of all, Robert McNamara of Ford and the Department of Defense. David Halberstam catches the flavor of that analytic ideal in this description of McNamara's style:

> *If the body was tense and driven, the mind was mathematical, analytical, bringing order and reason out of chaos. Always reason. And reason supported by facts, by statistics—he could prove his rationality with facts, intimidate others. Once, sitting at CINPAC for eight hours, watching hundreds and hundreds of slides flashed across the screen . . . he finally said, after seven hours, "Stop the projector. This slide number 869 contradicts slide 11." Slide 11 was flashed back and he was right. They did contradict each other. . . . Everyone was in awe.*[8]

Robert McNamara became something of an idol of the analytic management movement, and with reason. McNamara and his colleagues were brilliant, dedicated executives who helped push their institutions to new levels of excellence and efficiency—at a price.

AM's growth was also tied to the arrival of the computer. In 1951, Remington Rand's UNIVAC I had become operational. By 1954, there were still probably fewer than ten computers—multi-vacuum-tubed monsters—in place in the United States.[9] The implications of that brand new information technology, however, took a few years to catch on. Even in 1957, for example, a pioneering colleague, Allen Newell, gave a clear and lucid talk about the nature of computers to my class of middle managers at Carnegie Tech. He had a hard time. "Pie in the sky! Send that guy back to his cave!" the students said to me afterward. "What have those weird machines got to do with managing?" The following year, however, when Allen gave a similar talk, there was standing room only. By then, it seemed, corporate America had awakened to the computer's potential, especially its potential for supporting the nascent drive toward analytic management.

Old hierarchies took to this analytic approach much more quickly than they had taken to participation. AM was high on measurement and control. It promised to reinforce the old hierarchical structure by further differentiating ranks and levels and by replacing many humans with more reliable new machines. Even AM's initial label, Management Science, sounded eerily familiar, like Taylor's *Scientific Management* spelled backward and all natted up in suit and tie.

Like participative management, analytic management is more than a methodology. It is also something of a faith. Its true believers tend to treat systematic analysis as *the* route to organizational Eden. While participative management's advocates were trying to figure out the best psychological solutions to organizational problems, AM's practitioners were busy calculating the most logical, and therefore "correct," solutions. Then, having figured out the right answers, they tended to tell others, usually line middle managers, to step forward and implement them.

It was at this point, as an earlier chapter suggested, that some of AM's difficulties began. The "I-decide-it-then-you-do-it" posture can even now generate high tension in large organizations, especially among working line managers. Systemizing analysts, focused on the rationally best way to get things done, are upset when people who don't belong to the AM church act "resistant." One example: the deep psychological rift during the Vietnam era between McNamara's DOD planners and officers in the field. That was when body counts, tailored to please HQ, were often "not exactly" correct. The second war with Iraq appears to have generated somewhat similar distortions in communication between the Pentagon and field commanders.

The Era of the Analytic M.B.A.

For business schools, AM was manna from heaven. Back then, most American business schools (there weren't many anywhere else) ranked somewhere south of physical education. In the early 1950s, for example, as sophisticated a place as the University of Chicago's Graduate School of Business was still offering courses in business letter writing. So AM's push toward quantification and rigor was just what B-school deans needed to buy them some academic respectability. Moreover, the Ford and Carnegie Foundations, seeking to vivify management education, put several million dollars behind analytic-style management education. That certainly helped.

AM's favorite word, *analysis,* quickly became the buzzword of the business school revolution. One course after another slipped that word into its title: Marketing Analysis, Operations Analysis, Systems Analysis, Financial Analysis, Strategic Analysis. B-schools began churning out hordes of analytically trained, by-the-numbers M.B.A.'s, an overkill that eventually led to the derisive epithet—usually applied to recent B-school grads—"paralysis by analysis."

Nevertheless, by the 1970s the M.B.A. had become a moderately respectable and increasingly popular academic degree. Between 1960 and 2000, the population of American M.B.A.'s exploded from a mere 4,400 graduates per annum to 112,000.[10] Western organizations added hordes of these young systemizers to their managerial ranks. Newly minted M.B.A.'s thus became major carriers of analytic management's systemizing virus, infecting organizations everywhere. Numerically adept but often relationally gauche, these numbers-oriented young people headed mostly toward arm's-length jobs as staff planners, financial analysts, or outside-the-walls consultants. From these tactical positions, they further complicated the lives of working middle managers.

The Disconnect Between AM and PM

Participative management and analytic management both prospered, but they certainly didn't hit it off with each other. PMs were humanizers. AMs were systemizers. Their cognitive styles were very far apart.

Systemizing AMs treated human feelings and emotions as flaws, noise that interfered with the smooth workings of the system. If the Lord had designed humans properly, AMs tended to think, She would have enlarged their heads and shrunk their hearts. But for participative types, these same feelings and emotions were the essence of it all, the stuff of which morale, motivation, and even creativity were made.

From an AM perspective, a good decision was the analytically best decision—the correct answer. From the participative perspective, a good decision meant something quite different. It meant an answer that real people would willingly, even enthusiastically, carry out—a workable answer. In practice, as every manager (and politician) knows, correct answers and workable answers are often miles apart.

But more was yet to come.

HOT GROUPS: JUST DOING IT

In the 1980s, a new style came riding into town, hootin' and hollerin' and kickin' up a storm. These hyperactive new kids—the irreverent, ebullient high-tech start-ups of Silicon Valley—began to elbow their way into the organizational family. And they weren't polite about it. They thumbed their noses at everyone in sight. They scorned "silly" bureaucratic requirements. Progress reports and regular working hours were not their thing. They shied away from touchy-feely participation. They viewed number-driven analytic management as an alien from a distant galaxy. And they didn't like command-and-control hierarchies *at all.*

Were these kids just a new variety of systemizers? They could think analytically, but analysis was not at the core of their game. Doing the impossible was. Were they humanizers? They didn't like hierarchies, but they were anything but touchy-feely types. For them, it was all in the task—an intrinsic, intellectual dedication to solving fascinating problems. In their hot little world, the challenging task was king—not loving relationships, not mathematical models, and certainly not hierarchies.[11]

At first, the big old boys trivialized these newcomers, ridiculing their tattered blue jeans, weird working hours, and diets of pizza and Coke. These youngsters (by the mid-1980s, the average age of Apple's people had climbed worrisomely high—to twenty-six!)

weren't *real* executives, and their messy little outfits weren't *real* organizations. But they were great open-field runners. They could move fast, reverse, invent, spot openings, and dive into them. And very often they really did the impossible.

Of course, such unmannerly behavior wasn't most large organizations' cup of tea. But how long could they ignore these nerdy youngsters? They were disrupting everything, initiating the information age, and thereby speeding up the metabolisms of even the most lethargic giants. Their "children's crusade" (a phrase often lobbed at them like a hand grenade) finally forced the big guys to think the unthinkable. They, too, might have to put speed, flexibility, and innovativeness at the top of their wish lists, even above their classic Holy Grails of orderliness and productivity.

Furthermore, Lockheed's development of its "skunk works" several decades earlier had demonstrated how such hot groups could work even in a large organization and not only with youngsters.[12] That set an example for other large technical companies, and thence for some non-tech organizations, too. The time had come for large hierarchies to hang hot groups' faded blue jeans alongside analytic button-downs and participative pink jumpsuits.

Small, Hot Organizations Cool Down

There is an irony here. As big, orderly hierarchies struggle to adopt the style of little hot groups, some of the little groups grow larger, and, of course, they all grow older. Eventually these two forces—growth and the aging process—do their irreversible work. They begin to drag the now-adolescent little guys into the hierarchical morass. The open doors of their wild and wonderful cultures begin to close. Their task-impassioned heat begins to cool. Territorial conflicts and power struggles erupt. Half-truths and untruths multiply. Competition trounces collaboration. Cynicism increases, as do all the other disruptive camp followers of creeping hierarchy.

Such transformation from small, agile, task-obsessed groups to heavy-handed hierarchy is seldom intentional, yet it happens. But a caveat here: Those rowdy young cultures, like all strong cultures, don't just curl up and die, at least not for a long time. They may get pushed into the organizational periphery, but even from there they can make lots of trouble for the suits who have been called in to run the grown-up show.

Here's an example of the early stages of such a clash, between a rapidly growing hot group culture and the hierarchical forces that were just beginning to tame it: Back in the mid-1980s, I gave a talk at a conference of Apple Computer's financial executives, presumably their most number-crunching, systemizing money managers. Here are some of my edited notes about that visit:

Suited and necktied, arrived at resort hotel outside of Phoenix just after dark. Met by an Apple person in full cowboy regalia. Immediately presented me with (1) a cowboy hat and (2) a yo-yo with picture of Albert Einstein on each side. Then driven, in a microbus, over dirt roads to a desert hilltop. Huge bonfire blazing. Masses of people milling around, dancing, shouting, eating, and drinking. Removed tie and jacket. Band playing bluegrass—loudly. On rough stage, turbaned Sikh acting as MC. Learned later he was financial manager of Apple's Singapore operation. Nothing like the sedate, well-mannered Singaporeans I knew.

At 3 A.M., party going full blast. Began to worry. Scheduled to speak in five hours, at 8 A.M. Searched for a ride back to the hotel. Finally found reluctant driver. Clear he felt I was a terrible party pooper.

Caught a three-hour nap. Arrived at appointed conference room just before 8, expecting audience of perhaps five sleepy people. Instead the place was jammed. Crowd bubbling and lively, gulping coffee and chatting animatedly in little groups. During my spiel, most didn't sit in available chairs. Some stood, some squatted on the floor, some were lying down. Made my presentation. Surprisingly, they listened. Asked good questions and debated relevant issues.

John Sculley, the CEO, was just arriving as I finished. Hung around to listen to his talk. Sculley, lucidly and sincerely, tried to convince audience that Apple needed to get organized. Talked about budgets, controls, stockholders, and marketing. Several in audience (and these were financial managers!) rose to complain.

They hadn't come to Apple to worry about stock prices and market-ing strategies. They'd come to build computers for the millions. Loud applause—for complainers, not for Sculley.[13]

The inevitable confrontation had begun: the clash between that hot group culture's passion and the steadily increasing pressures to tighten and regularize the company's processes. Since then, some might say, Apple has "matured." It is no longer a callow youth. Others probably view the new Apple as a conventionalized, beaten-down shadow of its once free, unhaltered past. Despite all these changes, however, Apple is still Apple. It may not be as wide open as it used to be, but it's not IBM. Cultures, like hierarchies, die hard.

One more point: When small, egalitarian organizations mature and move toward hierarchy, the outcomes aren't all bad. With maturity come other attributes: stability, self-discipline, and thoughtfulness. Today's *Wall Street Journal* suggests that Cisco may be undergoing such a conversion—a somewhat late-in-life conversion—from a hot group mentality to a more mature, and perhaps more hierarchical, one. Cisco, the piece says, is now attacking "a huge waste of time and people":

A Cisco executive rooting for slower growth? That would have been heresy in the Silicon Valley of the 1990s. But this is not the old Cisco. . . . The old Cisco favored speed and internal competition; the new Cisco emphasizes deliberation and teamwork. The old Cisco devoured startups and raced to build niche products; the new Cisco wants to create fewer, more versatile products internally. The old Cisco tried to do everything; the new Cisco is trying to figure out what to do.[14]

Slowing down once in a while isn't always a bad idea!

DIGESTING THE THREE CHANGES

As these three changes moved into big hierarchical organizations— participation from the humanizing side, analytic management from the systemizing side, and hot groups mostly from out of the blue—they bumped into one another, like incoming, outgoing, and criss-crossing waves on the ocean's shore. Instead of a smooth transition into a new organizational equilibrium, we got a new disequilibrium, a mishmash of conflicting ways of managing—some of them support-ive of the existing hierarchical structure, others tending to undermine it. In most cases, they have not even yet come together to form a coherent whole. And middle managers were usually the ones who got the job of making a neat, integrated system out of all of them.

How can organizations live with such multiple, mutually contra-dictory pressures? Quite easily. Unlike some of us individuals, large organizations are extremely good at rubbing their bellies and patting their heads at the same time. They can go off in several directions at once without even being aware that they're doing so. What helps them perform such marvelous tricks is their basic, immutable hierar-chical architecture. It keeps the whole shebang from flying apart. For despite those three concubines—participation, analysis, and task-impassioned groups—the hierarchy remains First Wife. Each of the newcomers must still curtsy before her and adapt to her ways.

Modern managers may do more participative-style listening, dele-gating, and sharing, but they—individually—are still held account-able by those up the hierarchy for the decisions they make and the results they achieve. Analytic strategists can come up with answers they *know* are analytically correct, but they can't get them imple-mented without upstairs approval. And little, internal, hot groups—skunk works and the like—may operate hierarchy-free for short periods, but some powerful seniors must back them up and hold off inquisitors long enough for them to do their things.

Big organizations can live with these multiple options, but indi-vidual managers have trouble juggling them. Managing participa-tively, for example, doesn't mix well with hierarchy's traditional top-down command and control style, and managing by the numbers may interfere with participative style. Too many interdependent choices can even be a bit crazy-making. They can complicate mana-gerial life relative to the simple, old, any-color-as-long-as-it's-black authoritarian style.

IN SUMMARY

Since the 1950s, at least three major managerial changes have made their way into large hierarchies: humanizing participative management in the 1950s, systemizing analytic management a bit later, and small hot groups in the late 1970s and the 1980s. These three entries, this chapter has proposed, have piled into the old hierarchy, but not always in a coherent, coordinated way. Even now, inside many organizations, the three tend to bang up against one another and against the dominating hierarchy, too. Or, conversely, they may simply pass one another in the night, each doing its own thing without much awareness of the others. Such happenings should lead to chaos, but mostly they don't. The overarching hierarchy and its dedicated middle managers are there to help hold together the whole diverse, squabbling family.

That's what chapter 5, the last chapter of part II, is about: how hierarchical organizations try to use their managers to help them ingest and digest those diverse innovations and still get their work done.

FIVE

How Big Hierarchies Cope with Change

We tend to stereotype big organizations as though they were all alike—ponderous, lumbering, unresponsive dinosaurs. That just isn't so. Some deserve the tag, behaving as though they still lived in the Mesozoic era, permitting others more fleet of mind to speed past them. Familiar names such as McDonnell Douglas, Westinghouse, LTV, and Kmart have been cannibalized by even bigger fish, or have otherwise come close to going belly-up. Still others—for example, Montgomery Ward, born in 1872—have simply given up the ghost. But let's not forget that some brash, young organizations, such as Enron (b.1982), have also imploded—not from moving too slowly, but from trying to move so fast that they overheated and burned.

Many big, old organizations, in fact, have shown themselves to be as innovative and adaptive as any of the small, fast-moving youngsters. Some have been in the forefront of innovation, alert enough to change themselves well before their environments forced change upon them. Their size and enormous financial resources have permitted them to undertake leading edge experiments that would have risked the very lives of smaller, poorer organizations. Indeed, many large, mature companies—DuPont (b.1802), Royal Dutch Shell (b.1833), Nokia (b.1865), Nestlé (b.1867), GE (b.1890), 3M (b.1902), IBM (b.1911), Sony (b.1946), and Intel (b.1968—just a young adult), along with many others—have kept up with the times, at least until now.

Will these successful adapters continue to prosper? Perhaps, or perhaps not. Multiple and complex factors determine organizations' fates, just as they do our own. We should have learned by now that it is presumptuous to believe that we can foretell organizations' futures. But it remains indisputable that many large, old organizations, in the past and in the present, have innovated and adapted with the best of them.

When, for example, the participative management movement got under way in the 1950s, some of the world's largest companies were among its first adopters. By the early 1960s, Standard Oil had sent every manager from its Baton Rouge refinery to spend two weeks off-site immersed in that radical new technique, sensitivity training. That was neither a trivial risk nor a trivial investment. Earlier (1956), GE had created what it still calls "the first major corporate business school" at Crotonville, New York. European giants, such as Nestlé, Royal Dutch Shell, and Unilever, were not far behind. It's also worth noting that GE's business school was started three years *before* the nearly simultaneous publications of the Ford Foundation's Gordon and Howell report and the Carnegie Corporation's Pierson report on business education. Those studies initiated the American (and worldwide) business school revolution.

How, then, can massive hierarchies manage to innovate and change and yet maintain their basic hierarchical form? Following are some of the ways. Notice that each of the options can have major effects on the behaviors the organization will then expect from its managers and on behaviors it is likely to reward or punish.

PICK A CARD, JUST ONE CARD

Consider the three changes described in chapter 4: participative management, analytic management, and hot groups. A few large organizations have tried to integrate all three by simply choosing one of them and making it king of the hill, pushing the others into ancillary positions.

That's what ITT did during the reign of its somewhat infamous leader Harold Geneen. ITT went the systemizing, analytic management route. Managing-by-the-numbers clearly ruled its roost. If you had been an executive in Geneen's kingdom, you would have learned, early on, that you had better have the hard facts at your fingertips, and they'd better be right. Once, for example, after we had been discussing ITT in an executive class, one participant came up for a private talk. "I just want to tell you," he said, "that I used to work for Geneen. To say he managed by the numbers was the least of it. None of us slept the nights before we had to present our monthly reports. When that moment arrived, we were all seated around the boss's big mahogany conference table trying to look calm. Then came his hard, cold cross-examination. You just prayed that you'd covered all the bases and that your numbers checked out. If not . . ."

That executive's description sounded much like some French colleagues' description of what oral doctoral exams used to be like at the Sorbonne. Only there you didn't sit around a table. You stood, all alone, your friends (and enemies) arrayed in a semicircle behind you, while your black-robed board of examiners glowered down at you from a mile-high rostrum. That ordeal came only once in a lifetime. The ITT torture chamber happened again and again.

Nevertheless, however unpleasant and anxiety provoking, the ITT culture was strong and clear. Whatever the pain, managers all down the line knew the priorities. Other ways of operating took secondary positions. That manager told me, at the end of our conversation, that he had quit ITT. Knowing the ITT culture and knowing himself, he had decided that it was not the place for him. When the gap between what an organization expects and what a particular manager is willing to give becomes too great, it's time for a divorce.

Contrast ITT with Hewlett-Packard. HP, too, developed a single-minded, clearly focused culture. But it picked its own humanizing, participative option. There, participation, not the numbers, played the starring role. The company's central maxim was the humanistic "HP Way." To make sure that everyone was imbued with the cultural norm, HP regularly brought its overseas managers to Palo Alto for several weeks of immersion in the HP Way. That humanizing culture worked very successfully for decades. Of course, even there, the hierarchical music always played softly in the background.

Consider a third, somewhat younger organization, Apple Computer. It would be inaccurate to claim that it *chose* the third card, a very hot groupy kind of culture. Rather, the culture simply grew as an extension of the lifestyles of the founding group. At Apple, in those early years, even the hierarchy played a minor role. Small, impassioned groups, challenged by their tasks, were at the heart of it all.

Each of these three companies opted for a different dominant way of coping with change. In each, its choice worked—for a while. Monday morning quarterbacks can properly point out that emphasizing only one option and downplaying the others eventually led to trouble. People were hurt at ITT, and Geneen's massive and rather bloated conglomerate was quickly cut down to size by his successor. HP, after several decades of great success, fell behind in the rapidly accelerating information business. Critics asserted that its revered humanistic HP Way was holding it back, that it lacked the necessary agility and competitive killer instinct. So change was imposed on HP the old-fashioned way, by the exercise of power. And Apple changed, too, after suffering something of a near-death experience, apparently caused by a lack of disciplined coordination and tight controls. But Apple managed to make it through that crisis.

Although strong organizational cultures may change, it is worth reemphasizing that they are slow to fade completely away. Cultures—whether societal, tribal, or organizational—are not easily or quickly eradicated. The Soviets spent three-quarters of a century trying to eliminate the Russian people's bent for religion. They failed. Even when a large company's culture appears to be changing quite rapidly, the changes may be, in fact, more superficial than real. HP, for example, has, in recent years, been undergoing radical change. But do not expect the HP Way to go gently into a new hurry-up, numbers-oriented way of life. Its classic humanism may take a beating, but major aspects of the old culture are likely to hang on—and cause stresses ahead.

TO COPE WITH CHANGE, ISOLATE

Isolation is a double-duty tool. When large hierarchies feel a change coming on, they can apply the isolation tactic in either of two ways. They can use it defensively, to block the change and protect the status quo. Alternatively, they can apply the same tactic offensively, to initiate change that they believe might not otherwise occur.

Defensive Isolation

Sometimes ideas for change (and occasionally demands for change) begin with a small group deep inside a large hierarchy. That group may be convinced that its great idea will solve some key problems. So it proselytizes, trying to persuade the rest of the organization to accept its new method or process or product. Such evangelical inside groups almost always run into trouble. They keep annoying the rest of the parent organization. Resistance builds, conflict erupts. Eventually the parent must take action.

For centuries, large organizations have tried to cope with pressures from such "dissident" groups by isolating them, physically or psychologically or both. When an irritating internal group becomes too bothersome, a big hierarchy may do what the Wicked Queen did to Snow White. It ships the little troublemaker off to the forest (or assigns it an irrelevant task) where it can no longer cause trouble. Perhaps the group will prosper in its new surroundings, in which case the parent can take both the credit and the profit. Or the group may fail and dissolve as the hot issue that spawned it fades from the headlines.

Five hundred years ago the leaders of the Carmelite Order in Spain tried to use that isolation tactic with Saint Theresa of Avila and her troublesome little band of discalced Carmelites. Theresa's group felt that her order's ethical standards had deteriorated, and Theresa kept saying so, quite loudly. To get her out of their hair, the order's leaders sent her to a far-off convent out in the boonies. But that indefatigable woman did not fade away. Even from her isolation, she organized another protest group and managed to enlist the patronage of King Philip II of Spain. Her group grew. Finally, Rome forced the Carmelites to ease their pressures against Theresa.

Eventually, they did an about-face, absorbing her group back into the mainstream until, finally, she was canonized.[1]

A few hundred years later, just before World War II, the U.S. Army Air Corps used a somewhat similar defensive tactic. It tried to isolate and then break up General Claire Chennault's Flying Tigers, an autonomous, highly effective volunteer group of ragtag pilots who flew for Chiang Kai-shek against the Japanese.[2] Thanks to the intrusion of two patrons—Mme. Chiang and President Franklin Roosevelt—the effort to isolate the Flying Tigers didn't work very well, so the Air Corps also made a U-turn and tried to absorb the unit in order to control it. That didn't work either. The Flying Tigers did finally become part of the U.S. military, under General Joe Stilwell, but in a manner that allowed them to retain most of their autonomy and style.

Isolating Offensively

Turn now to the more positive side of the isolation tactic: intentionally isolating a group in order to effect change in a large hierarchy. When a stodgy organization wants to undertake an innovative, experimental project, it may have the good sense to acknowledge its own stodginess—that it is set up to perform normal routines well enough but is not designed for radical innovating. So it identifies a small, special group and gives it unfettered freedom to do its offbeat thing. That's what Xerox did when it wisely set up Palo Alto Research Center (PARC) in Silicon Valley, nearly three thousand miles from home. There, in splendid isolation—but close to the relevant action—that quasi-autonomous group would be able to create and invent the office of the future in its own way. This arrangement would provide the best of all worlds. The home organization wouldn't be disturbed by the disruptive little group, nor would it be envious of the special treatment PARC was receiving. And the offshoot group would not be stymied by the usual bureaucratic controls.

The isolation format can work very well. Apple used it successfully to develop the Macintosh, and IBM did it to develop its PC. There is, however, one important caveat: The formula will work only if it includes a clear exit strategy. At some point, the small, innovating group and the large, rather closed hierarchy must reconnect. If child and parent have been separated for too long, they may no longer even acknowledge each other. That's the point at which Xerox's problem arose. There was no channel for reintegrating PARC's good work into the main corpus of the organization.

A delicate and critical balance point lies somewhere between too much isolation and too little. Isolated groups can easily lose contact with the needs of colleagues, customers, and other relevant constituencies. Conversely, parent organizations, largely ignorant of what isolated groups are doing, may bypass or ignore the isolates' work or may, by then, have gone off in some different direction. When such creative groups finally emerge from their cocoons, bearing their innovative surprises, the parent hierarchy is likely to be less than thrilled. Large organizations seldom like surprises. Surprises disturb hierarchical good order and routine. At that point, the group, originally established to generate change, becomes—from the parent's perspective—something of a pariah, a disruptive rather than a creative force.

Variants of the isolation method are quite common, as are the mixed results. Large companies, for example, frequently conduct organizational development or leadership seminars off-site, on "cultural islands." There, in temporary seclusion, participants can work with intense concentration and without distraction. The workshop's impact can thus be maximized. The trouble usually starts at the dangerous next step: transition back home. That difficult point even has a name. It's called "the reentry problem." That's when the seminar participants—turned on and eager to put their new learning to work—return to their normal jobs, only to bump into the great, gray miasma of "normal" hierarchical routines. Instead of a grand welcome home, they are likely to be greeted by desks piled high with accumulated work, brush-offs from their too-busy peers, and icy frowns from their bosses. Within a few weeks, much of their newly acquired learning and their enthusiasm for propagating it begin to fade away.

TO COPE WITH CHANGE, MATRIX

I chatted recently with an experienced engineer, a program manager from a large aerospace company. He is in charge of major structural components being built for a new space station. He works pretty much by himself, he told me. He has no direct reports, even though he's "responsible" for a program worth many hundreds of millions of dollars. His company is *matrixed,* so, although he has great responsibilities, he has little formal authority. There are no stars on his shoulders. Yet he must coordinate the work of many specialized groups and work closely with the project's customers. His job, he said, requires a lot of persuasion and negotiation.

It seemed like an interesting setup, so I pressed him to learn more. "I report to a vice-president," he told me, "and he reports to the president."

"You have nobody reporting to you, and you're only two levels down from the top of a huge organization?" I asked. "That seems an unusually flat structure."

"Well, not quite," he replied. "My president reports to a group president, who reports to an area president, who reports to the corporate CEO."

Usually, in matrixed organizations, individual managers have two (or more) bosses: one from a discipline, and another from a particular project, and that split often causes trouble. This engineer mentioned only one boss, and he had no direct reports, so his job sounded much like a product manager's job. His organization, then, is certainly hierarchical, but it is tempered by what he called a matrix inserted within—or, rather, beneath—the old systemizing hierarchical umbrella. The matrix was laid on to help the organization handle the increasing complexities of its tasks, to improve horizontal communication, and to speed the other interactions needed to knit together complicated projects.

His position requires this program manager to operate mostly in humanizing, egalitarian ways. He cannot rely on his rank or authority to get the job done, at least not very much. Nor can he rely on that other option, an internal market. Our program manager cannot offer to pay the metallurgy group a higher price to do its part of his work faster or better. Instead, he must depend heavily on his ability to establish positive relationships with a multitude of other groups. Of course, he must also be pretty good at juggling schedules and the like, but interpersonal skills are vital to his success.

True, our program manager does not have to rely entirely on such social skills, because the hierarchy is still there to back him up. If he really has trouble getting the metallurgists to do their part, he can always resort to his fallback: He can call for help from a higher authority, from his boss upstairs. But he'd better not do that very often, not if he wants high performance ratings.

Those who have worked within matrixed organizations will doubtless attest that they are far from ideal tools. They are a kind of quasi-humanizing mechanism installed inside systemizing hierarchies to help them cope with complexity, but without seriously shaking up the hierarchy. Notice, too, that matrixes help "solve" difficult problems by handing them off to middle managers such as our program manager. They ask managers to pull everything together by exercising "influence without authority." Nudged along by a combination of human goodwill, interpersonal skill, a sense of common purpose, and appropriately injected pressures from upstairs, matrixes can help hierarchical organizations cope with change. They make the middle manager's job quite difficult and probably quite challenging as well. And they operate *under* the hierarchy, not in place of it.

COPING WITH INCOMING CHANGE: OTHER OPTIONS

Suppose our company has bought into all three managerial changes—participation, analytic management, and hot groups—and into other major technological and social changes as well. It would be great if we could really blend them all together, squeezing the best from each one while maintaining a reasonable degree of harmony among all of them. Some organizations actually come close to doing that, although it's probably fair to say that most have trouble. Conflicts break out. Policies don't trickle down—or up—as they're supposed to. So big hierarchies also try to handle difficult incoming changes in other ways. Here are a few of those ways.

Act Small, Even When You're Big

How can an organizational elephant match the speed and agility of a nimble little organizational fox? Both participation and hot groups work best in the small, not in the large. Great armies are anathema to both of them. So one way to get the best from these styles is to replace the elephant with a collection of foxes.

GE, under Jack Welch, may not have broken itself into small autonomous pieces, but it did make *acting small* one of its two explicit goals: "To revolutionize this company to have the speed and agility of a small enterprise."[3] During its early glory years, HP also tried to keep the advantages of smallness even as the corporation grew large. Here's a 1958 item from HP's autobiographical Web site: "Any group that grows to 1,500 people is divided with the resulting groups having their own profit-and-loss accountability. This decentralization allows the company to react to changing conditions, move quickly and get away from an overly bureaucratic structure."[4]

Smaller units, of course, mean more total units. Many modern organizations do just that, violating an old hierarchical "principle": that the span of control must never exceed the magic number seven. These companies build flatter, multiunit, "federalist" hierarchies with spans of control a great deal larger than seven. They also make more use of temporary teams. Until recently, the Swiss/Swedish multinational ABB was frequently cited as an example of such a federalized structure, but at this writing it appears to have retreated from that model.[5] Still, even within large hierarchies, when it comes to dealing with rapid change, small can be beautiful.

Formalize and Depersonalize

This is the most venerable approach to change—or rather to the avoidance of change. It is an approach long associated with traditional hierarchies. The central principle: Let the organization be governed by fixed rules and defined roles, not by variable, less-than-rational humans. Let it be stable and unchanging over long periods, as the world once seemed to be. That's essentially what some extreme methods of days gone by tried to do—to reduce human variability by standardizing human activities.

It was a bit like what happened to a neighbor of mine, the owner of a leather tanning company. He came stomping into our house one evening. He was in a rage. He had hired a consulting firm to help him find ways to cut costs. The consultants had come up with what they thought was a great idea, he told me, between spluttered curses. All he had to do, they had recommended, was to make sure that all the raw hides he purchased were of exactly the same size and shape!

It's difficult to eliminate variations among animal hides, and it's even harder to eliminate variations among living human beings.

You may recall a standard old five-part textbook definition of managing that had a similar depersonalizing flavor. Managing, those texts opined, is about five issues: planning, organizing, staffing, controlling, and a fifth that varied with the author. This rationalistic way of thinking about organizations was sometimes carried to an extreme, as this excerpt from a 1947 book, *Organization of Industry*, illustrates. The book, incidentally, was written by a senior executive of a large company and was used as a text in a graduate class at MIT.

Purpose:
   1. Organization is a means to more effective concerted endeavor.
Scope:
   2. Organization deals exclusively with individuals and their relations.
   3. Organized endeavor is no more than the sum of individual endeavors.
Precedence:
   4. Organization precedes endeavor.
   5. Organization precedes the selection of members of enterprise and determines the requirement thereof.
   6. Organization should determine the selection of personnel rather than personnel determine the nature of organization.[6]

The author then went on to lay out rules about responsibility (it "inheres exclusively in individuals"), authority ("In each responsibility is inherent an equivalent authority"), and so on. It was a valiant effort, although it now sounds a bit off the wall. But isn't much of that rather abstract way of thinking about organizing—charts, job descriptions, principles of authority and responsibility—still with us? It may be buried far beneath the modern organization's public face, but don't many such ideas remain deeply ingrained in the belief systems of even today's large hierarchical organizations? And perhaps also ingrained in our own individual belief systems?

That way of thinking treats the construction of an organization like the construction of a house. Once built, the finished organization is expected to remain largely intact, unchanging, stably fixed to its foundation for long periods. Portions may be remodeled every decade or two, but once the structure is built, serious change means, almost by definition, serious disruption.

Such depersonalized thinking drove some old organizations to build walled, moated fortresses, protective of the status quo, expecting the storms of change to pass, awaiting a return to a "normalcy" that would never come. That kind of thinking is obviously at odds with our turbulent, almost randomly changing world. Yet some large hierarchies continue to view things that way, and some of them have been so unable to adapt that they have simply passed away. But others have managed to break those bonds—or maybe their leaders never read the old textbooks.

Get Rid of Archaic Hierarchies

Perhaps this book is all nonsense. Perhaps the era of the old multilevel hierarchy really has reached its end. Perhaps, although they don't know it, those surviving hierarchies are really the last of their breed. Ergo, chuck 'em!

And replace them—with what?

Technologize

Hierarchical organizations have long carried on a complex love/hate affair with technology, much as they have with people. Corporations have been both technology's slave and its master. They need technology, lest more sophisticated competitors leapfrog them. They want it to help them cut costs, replace people, and develop new products. But they are also ensnared by it because they have no option except to keep up with it.

So to an ever-increasing extent, hierarchical organizations are trying to own and control technology. Increasingly, only they and government have the enormous resources required to keep it rolling ahead in the directions they want it to roll. It's true that cloistered, old, slow-moving universities—not aggressive corporations—have been the traditional wellsprings of science and technology. In the past, most great scientists were also professors—Galileo at Padua, Kepler at Graz, Newton at Cambridge. Most of the scientists who initiated technological revolutions have been nurtured in such academic shelters, often with no thought of practical utility, let alone of profit. Even now, universities remain the major sources of scientific discovery and hence of technological development. Of the thirty-one Nobel Prize winners in chemistry and physics between 1995 and 2000, only one worked at a private company (Texas Instruments). Three were employed at quasi-independent research institutes. The remaining twenty-seven were on university faculties.

But all that is changing fast. Corporations may be Johnny-come-latelies to the science and technology business, but they are powerful and fast-moving Johnny-come-latelies.[7] So they are trying to cope with the tidal wave of technological change by putting more resources—human and financial—into the race to keep up with it. And one disturbing and worrisome way many large organizations are doing that is by exercising greater financial control over university-based research.[8]

Another way is to pass more of the keeping-up challenge to their middle managers. For modern middle managers, accelerating technology is thus becoming both a blessing and a curse. Technology provides magic tools to help us attack previously intractable, even unimagined, problems, but it also provides Big Brother Hierarchy with the wherewithal further to tighten control over us. New and ever newer technology can free managers from laborious chores, but it can also add new, previously unforeseen ones. Technology can make managers and other workers obsolete well within their normal career spans. And technology can also push people aside, into ancillary roles, as it has often done in the past.

Nevertheless, for reasons good and bad, the race to technology will continue to accelerate. So, too, will technology's pressures on organizations, pressures that seem at least as likely to reinforce organizational hierarchies as to weaken them.

Just Get Rid of People

This one is really a corollary to the technologizing "solution." An earlier chapter suggested that hierarchies want to get rid of people at least as much as people want to get rid of hierarchies. It is people, those highly touted "most valuable assets," who cause many of organizations' troubles. So let's use modern technology to help us eliminate people.

That's hardly a new option. Organizations have been doing it, bit by bit, for a long, long time. Now, though, we may be approaching a paradigm shift. The serious possibility of simply getting rid of a large portion of us humans' brains—let alone our arms and legs—is coming closer to feasibility. Nor is it only a matter of sending both low- and high-tech jobs to places where people work more cheaply. It is again also a matter of shifting both high- and low-tech jobs to new kinds of machines, or even leapfrogging those jobs by inventing new technological methods and products.

Let Middle Managers Figure Things Out

Most corporate cultures aren't as clearly defined as ITT's or HP's or Apple's. Many haven't been able coherently to weave the three managerial changes into their organizational fabrics. So they "cope" by simply loading them onto the backs of middle managers.

Sometimes middle managers must sally forth to champion their division's preferred change and then fight for it against other units' manager/gladiators, who favor different changes. That's what reportedly was happening in 2001 and some years thereafter within the U.S. Government. Colin Powell's internationalist State Department and Donald Rumsfeld's more unilateralist Department of Defense were at odds on many policy issues. Insiders report that the real battle was being fought, not at the top, but several rungs down the hierarchy, by committed midlevel members of the two groups.

Such conflicts happen in big hierarchies all the time. The humanizing HR people may be trying hard to build more participation, while the systemizing finance folks are tightening controls and requiring more frequent progress reports. Similarly, small hot

groups, with their unusual ways and voracious demands for resources, almost always need to have some senior champions to hold
back the conservative forces that want to rein them in.

THE STRUGGLES WITHIN

The most difficult battles inside organizations are waged not between agents of warring units but rather inside the hearts and minds
of individual managers. For in most large hierarchies, it is middle
managers who must somehow integrate all three changes, and others as well. The wider world thrusts these changes upon the organization, and the organization relays them to the in-between folks for
implementation.

Of course, the organization promises to help. It gives its middle
managers epaulets of authority, but as chapter 6 will try to show,
authority isn't always a very useful tool. The company may arrange
for middle managers to take a leadership course or a management
science course at the university. But even though such courses may
be valuable in other ways, they probably won't be of much help as
managers struggle to integrate these various approaches.

Like it or not, middle managers have perforce become the acro-
bats of the big organizational circus, juggling the three managerial
changes and more, while tenuously balancing on their hierarchical
ladders.

IN SUMMARY

Big old hierarchical organizations have been much maligned. But
when it comes to keeping up with the changing world, many have
not missed the boat. Indeed, some have sailed the boat themselves,
leading exploratory voyages into innovation and change.

Big hierarchical organizations are also different from one another,
so it is not surprising that they deal differently with the changes
pressed upon them by their changing environments. Some choose
one style of managing and make it the dominant driver of their corporate cultures. Others resist by isolating difficult internal groups

whose members are demanding change. Still others isolate such groups for the opposite reason: to provide those groups with enough elbow-room to initiate change. Some large hierarchies introduce matrixes and other horizontally and diagonally linked substructures to help cope with increasing, multifaceted complexity. Others try to act small in order to gain speed and agility. Some have tried to minimize their own hierarchical forms, hoping thereby to become more flexible and to sense changes in their environments more quickly. Still others technologize as fast as they can, believing technology is the steroid that will make them strong, agile, and responsive. And a few may even look forward to the time when technology will solve their human problems by getting rid of most of their humans.

Many organizations do a good job of bringing new ideas into their organizational tents, but then they do a poor job of weaving those ideas into their cultures. Instead, they dump that grab bag of changes onto the laps of their middle managers, expecting them to integrate and implement the whole potpourri.

These vagaries of middle managerial life in big hierarchical organizations deserve more attention. So it is to the ups and downs of middle managing in big hierarchical organizations that part III will now take us.

Part Three

HIERARCHIES
AND THE MANAGER

*P*arts I and II of this book are about
human organizations, with the emphasis on organizations. Part III
turns to the other word in that pair, to the humans working in organizations. What do all these changes mean for the people who work inside
hierarchies, especially for that great clan called middle managers?
They're the ones who must implement the changes and get good work
done in their ever more complicated structures. Chapter 6 is about
authority. Hierarchical organizations allocate varying amounts of authority to their managers. This authority is intended to serve as a
major power tool to help managers influence, control, and direct business processes. It is also a tool with which people higher in the hierarchy
can hold those below them responsible for outcomes. If managers have
the authority, the traditional reasoning goes, they can legitimately be
held accountable for getting the job done.

Authority, moreover, has a special characteristic. Some portion of it
is not only allocated to managers it is also affixed to them. Managers
can't get rid of it, no matter how hard they may try. And authority's
inescapable presence sends important signals to those beneath, above,

and around the manager. These signals affect other people's expectations and their behavior. That's why no sensible manager can safely act as though he or she doesn't have authority.

Chapter 7 moves from that traditional concept of authority to the re-popularized concept of leadership. Authority, it seems clear, is no longer a sufficient tool to help middle managers implement all those crisscrossing organizational changes—not in today's high-tech world and not with today's high-expectation people. If authority won't do it, then is leadership the answer? Leaders can motivate and inspire without authority, can't they? They do it via their charisma, persuasiveness, and vision and through the confidence they generate. By becoming leaders, perhaps middle managers will be able to resolve the inconsistencies and complexities of work and life in modern organizations.

Can managers become manager/leaders? Chapter 8 says yes to that question. It offers a three-phase model of the managing/leading process, a model that aspiring managers might find helpful if they want to lead. In today's environment, middle managers need the qualities of effective leaders along with the qualities of effective managers, including the stars of authority.

But there's a problem with the "let's-turn-managers-into-leaders" idea. Aren't leaders people who make up their own minds and march to their own drummers? Are big organizations really ready for hierarchies full of manager/leaders? How does that idea fit with the dominant top-down organizational design? And how does it fit with those manager/leaders whose leaderly views may not jibe with those of the leader upstairs?

Chapter 9 raises some of the difficult and often quite personal issues that confront modern manager/leaders. It is partially a review, but it tries to do more than that. It is a reminder that managers at all levels bear responsibility for the welfare of their people, the morality of their organizations, and even the well-being of the larger communities in which they reside.

SIX

The Manager's Authority

On the day that you are dubbed a manager in an organizational hierarchy, one of the goodies you are almost certain to receive is *authority*. You may or may not be given a key to the executive washroom, but you will surely get your ration of authority. Some chunk of it is laid upon almost all managers, and it is probably the most fundamental, most controlling fact of their and your managerial lives.

That authority, Ms. or Mr. Manager, shapes your expectations, and it shapes other people's expectations even more. It sketches the outlines of what constitutes appropriate managerial behavior and sets implicit rules about how you will behave in times of crisis. It constrains the ways others up and down the hierarchy communicate with you, in spoken and written words and even in body language. It affects how others will respond to your most casual comments and your day-to-day moods. It influences their readiness to agree or disagree with your opinions and their readiness to implement your decisions. No matter how you feel about it and no matter how much it is downplayed in your organization, your authority is not trivial. It's big!

Of course, authority isn't the tool it used to be, not in our newly interconnected, knowledge-based world. Today's organizational hierarchies are more complicated than the old ones, more humanized and at the same time more systemized, more measurement-happy, and more carefully controlled. The people in modern organizations are more knowledgeable and have higher expectations than their predecessors. But authority is still a huge part of the game, and it still has its special and critical characteristic: Authority sticks like instant glue. Managers can't shuck it off, no matter how they may try. Wanted or not, authority is an inescapable reality of life in human hierarchies.

And yet authority, that basic fact of managerial life, is often slighted or ignored in writings about the managing process and in the educations of managers-to-be. Its influential omnipresence in human organizations is frequently obscured or denied. Indeed some modern managers go to great lengths to act as though they don't have the authority that everyone knows they have.

That's what the rest of this chapter is about: authority, the middle manager's double-edged sword. It's about what authority is and why managers must never forget that they have it and that others have more or less of it. It's also about how it can be used effectively—and misused—in modern hierarchical organizations.

MANAGERS LIVE AND BREATHE AUTHORITY

Let's begin with a quasi-syllogism that's as relevant now as it was a hundred years ago:

> *Large organizations are hierarchies.*
> *Hierarchies are authoritarian systems.*
> *Managers in hierarchies implement those authoritarian systems.*
> *Therefore managers in hierarchies must behave in authoritarian*
> *   ways.*
> *True or false?*

Most modern managers would probably have little trouble making the choice. They would doubtless choose *false*. They don't think of themselves as club-wielding, do-it-or-else authoritarians, and most of them really aren't. They're more likely to view themselves as *leaders*, supportive, even inspirational leaders of their organizational units. Leaders are what chapter 7 is about. Leaders are what many managers would like to become and what some already are. But unlike authority—a required course—leadership is a managerial elective.

So this chapter takes the other position on that syllogism. It proposes that the correct answer is *true*, that no matter how one may feel about it, authority is—in a complicated, convoluted way—at the heart of the managerial role. Overt authoritarian behavior may be out of favor in large organizations, but the underlying reality of managerial authority is still there. And all the people anywhere near you, Ms. or Mr. Middle Manager, know pretty well how much of it you have.

What Is Authority?

It's hard to define precisely what the word *authority* means, but for managers in big hierarchies, two things about it are clear: Authority is always there, and it's always about power. Authority is like my father's strap. When I was a kid, Papa used his strap on me only once, but you can bet I always knew he had it. These days, most managers use their authority as rarely as Papa used his strap, and they certainly don't flaunt it, but everyone knows it's there. Those higher in the hierarchy have the authority—as *The American Heritage Dictionary* puts it—to "exact obedience" from those lower down. That's rather a harsh phrase. Most managers don't try to exact obedience from other people. Yet that's clearly one of the most important aspects of the managing process: getting people to do what managers want them to do.

Of course, modern managers also use many other, more positive ways of influencing their people. Authority is not only the power to punish but also the power to reward. Managers' authority, like Papa's strap, is almost always accompanied by control over valued resources. Papa didn't only have a strap—he also had the wherewithal to hand out weekly allowances. He could take us fishing and to ballgames. Managers can pay off desired behavior with financial and many other rewards. That's another reason that the people who report to you, middle manager, are always quite aware of your authority.

And behind all these good things, in the shadowy background, hangs Papa's ever-present strap.

AUTHORITY EMPOWERS AND AUTHORITY ISOLATES

Experienced managers understand what rookie managers often don't: that their organizations have tattooed formal authority upon them. They know that authority clings to their managerial role as the skin clings to the body.

Veteran managers also know something else. They know that although their authority empowers them, it also isolates them. Their authority imposes an invisible barrier, an impenetrable wall that always partially separates them from those of lower and of higher rank. They know that they can never quite be just one of the girls or boys with their subordinates, nor with their superiors. No one has to tell experienced managers such things. They are quite aware that hierarchy distances them from those on the rungs above, although some don't seem to realize how much it also distances them from those on the rungs below.

New corporate managers aren't usually taught that authority lesson, at least not explicitly. But after a few stumbles, most of them learn the immutable reality of their authority over others and others' authority over them, even when they don't actively exercise their authority. Acknowledging authority's constant, albeit often invisible reality is a first step toward learning to deal comfortably with hierarchical authority's mixed bag of costs and benefits.

Here's a case in point, in which a young manager, with the blessings of his modern corporation, is taught how to use participative, non-authoritarian methods to manage and motivate his group. Later he discovers (or believes he has discovered) that even though his organization talks the humanizing, participative talk, it doesn't exactly walk the walk.

During an off-site seminar, three of us academics had been touting participative, collaborative management styles. The seminar's students were middle-level managers from a large technical company.

At least one attendee, a new department head, must have paid attention, because, when I encountered him some months later, he was furious at us. Here's what followed:

Mike, someone told me you're really mad at us. Is that true?

You bet it's true. You guys screwed me over. You sold me all that crap about giving people more responsibility, more elbow room. You told me not to sit on top of every detail, not to micromanage. You said I would be surprised at the results.

Yes, we did say things like that. Did you try it? What happened?

Oh, sure, I tried it, and it blew up in my face.

Did the people in your group perform badly? Did they disappoint you?

No, they were great. They worked like the devil. They had all kinds of good ideas.

Then what's the problem?

The problem isn't with my group. It's at the other end. When I went up in front of the executive committee, they quizzed me, like they always do, about every detail in my unit. But this time I didn't know the damn details! I looked like an idiot! You didn't warn me about that!

For Mike, using the new participative style with his own group simply didn't fit into his organization's overall authoritative model. To behave the way we had encouraged him to behave, he would have to violate that overarching corporate style. At least that's the way he saw it—and we should have had the good sense to foresee it.

We should have done much more than just warn Mike. In our eagerness to teach the human and productive advantages of participative management, we had ignored a more basic lesson—the simple but vital lesson that big human organizations are hierarchies, and human hierarchies are authoritarian systems. Perhaps we had ignored it because that truth, like the air around us, is so natural that we didn't pay attention to it, or perhaps we didn't want to acknowledge it.

Yet, whether novices or veterans, all managers must stay constantly alert to the reality that they breathe in an atmosphere of authority. You can feel it the moment you pass through any large corporation's doors. It is manifest even in the physical architecture and décor of corporate headquarters, in office sizes, even in carpeting. If we had taught more about that pervasive reality, perhaps this budding manager's experiment with participation would not have bumped into his organization's enveloping hierarchy of authority.

In hindsight, what were Mike's options? One was simply to ignore all our advice and return to micromanaging. Another was to seek some middle ground. Some Mikes, those with less personal integrity, might have tried faking it—talking participative talk while walking an authoritarian walk. Or perhaps he could have let his people in on the act, explaining to them that he needed the details because the bureaucracy upstairs demanded it. But Mike was no dummy, nor was he a moral weakling. If this new, nonauthoritarian style promised to generate both productivity and morale, he could neither sensibly nor decently reject it. Yet more traditional top-down behavior—or manipulative behavior—might get him far better performance evaluations.

Did he have other options? Later in this chapter we'll return to Mike and to the idea of authoritative presence.

AUTHORITARIANISM: THE GORILLA WAITING IN THE WINGS

In our enlightened era, blatant use of authority is pretty much out of favor. Hierarchies' authoritarianism clashes with our larger society's democratic values, so most organizations do everything they can to obscure their authoritarian natures. Some do a pretty good job of dressing up to look like egalitarian democracies, and a few do it so well that they even convince themselves. But they're not democracies, and their managers know it. If they don't know it, they'd better learn it quickly.

Rookie managers such as Mike are apt to feel vaguely troubled by such contradictions. Their companies keep sending them conflicting signals. They ship their Mikes off to humanizing, antiauthoritarian training seminars about "team building," "active listening," and "coaching" to learn all sorts of humanizing skills. In this and other ways, they so obscure their organization's underlying authoritarian base that some beginning managers think that, like a clear glass door, it isn't really there—until they collide with it.

For no matter how glossed over it may be, hierarchical authority *is* there, always. Like a fish's water, authority is the manager's encompassing and constant medium, subtly shaping every facet of managerial behavior. Long ago the *Catholic Encyclopedia* put it rather precisely: "The 'Hierarcha' [read 'middle manager'] . . . is he who . . . both obeys and commands, but does not obey those he commands."[1] Of course, modern managers have much more wiggle room than those "hierarchas." They have space to speak out against commands they think are wrong, and space to listen downward to protests and ideas from their people. Yet, both upside and down, authority is always in the act.

Should We Assess the Worth of Human Beings?

Many managers, Mike included, don't feel good about this organizational squeeze. Like most of us, they've been raised in a democracy and hold strong egalitarian values. They don't view authoritarian methods as either moral or effective ways of dealing with their fellow human beings, and, at least on the surface, their organizations appear to feel the same way. So everything is made to look copasetic—until managers run up against the other side of hierarchy's split personality. Suddenly they are told that they must lay off three of the people on their team, the people with whom they have developed, as their organizations urged them to, close working relationships and warm, almost-family ties. Next, they encounter smarmy performance appraisals. Now they must divide their people into thirds and tell each member of the lowest third why he or she is way down there. It's something like being ordered to tell your eight-year-old twins that you love one of them a lot less than you love the other.

Many young people, when they move into managerial positions, experience a vague sense of dissonance about all this. A certain discomfort sneaks up on them, often without their recognizing its cause. They suffer as they carry out ritual performance appraisals on their subordinates, and they suffer again from the pain inflicted by their superiors' periodic appraisals of them. Solutions—such as the HR department's conversion of last year's 360-degree feedback plan into this year's new performance appraisal scheme—may provide bandages, but such devices are not likely to solve the real problem.

Nor has the problem been solved by any of the other systemizing solutions that, over the past half-century, have entered and then quickly exited the organizational domain. Back in 1957, Douglas McGregor published a now classic article called "An Uneasy Look at Performance Appraisals." In it he detailed some of the many difficulties generated by appraisal schemes.[2] Almost half a century later, in 2000, *HRFocus* magazine noted that the uneasiness continues unabated. At a Conference Board meeting of HR executives, 90 percent were less than satisfied with their companies' current appraisal systems.[3] Could that be because many of us feel a deep-down unease about evaluating the worth of other people? And about having to tell them (or be told) those evaluations face-to-face? Although we know full well that total egalitarianism is a fantasy, we also tend to honor our society's faith that no person is inherently worth more or less than any other.

Board members and CEOs are people, too. They share our cultural values, so many try to do more than simply sweep their organizations' authoritarianism under the rug. They work hard to reduce authority's relevance. They build organizations that push authoritarianism far into the background and more democratic behavior far forward so that their managers are seldom forced to confront the split. They focus the organization's energies on task more than procedure and on doing the job right more than on the right way of doing it. But they can never go all the way. Even managers in the most enlightened organizations periodically find themselves trapped between their personal values and their organization's immutable authoritarianism. That antidemocratic quality of hierarchical authority is like a pebble in the manager's shoe. It doesn't cause acute pain, but it's uncomfortable and irritating, and sooner or later we must do something about it.

A few managers in large organizations don't even perceive the dilemma, let alone suffer from it. They don't worry about behaving "democratically." Instead of feeling conflicted, they revel in their authority, taking personal pleasure in giving orders and even in receiving them. When people travel too far down that road, they become what researchers have called "authoritarian personalities."[4] Most such people eventually stir up so much hostility that they finally—and "finally" may take a long time—get into trouble. They simply cannot muster even the minimal social support they need to survive. In organizations, people need people, now more than ever.

Here's a case in point: I was recently invited to lunch with the CEO of a small technical company and the chairman of his board. This is the problem they thought I might be able to help them with: The most creative, productive, and professionally respected technical manager in their company, they said, had an extremely "difficult" personality. But he was also the guy who brought in more contracts than any of the rest of their people. He was given to fits of temper and sarcasm. He regularly put down the people who worked for him and his other colleagues. He often shouted that this employee or that one was a "fool" or an "incompetent" in front of many others. He was tearing up the place so much, the CEO said, that several other valuable employees were threatening to quit rather than "take any more of that crap." Yet Henry was so effective in his work that this young, growing, quite low-authoritarian company might well be in serious trouble without him.

The CEO and the chairman wanted to know what I thought of their tentative solution, a solution that, like their company, was technical—in this case, chemical. They wanted me to help talk Henry into going on a regimen of Prozac. They felt that might quiet him down. I said no. I had never met Henry, and I didn't want to talk to him about that. So they went ahead without me.

I don't know whether or not their solution worked. My bet is that it didn't. Sooner or later, I felt, that CEO would have to exercise his authority and choose between his organization and that valuable, but extremely divisive, individual.

AUTHORITARIAN DEMOCRATS: AN OXYMORON?

Plenty of organizations' leaders have hung on to the moral high ground, among them a number of valiant *authoritarian democrats,* executives who have actively and consciously used their authority to build low-authoritarian institutions. We mentioned them briefly earlier, and now they are worth a closer look.

Some companies regularly make *Fortune* magazine's list of "The 100 Best Companies to Work For."[5] I used that list as a small database in an earlier chapter. But how do such companies get that way? One of the most common routes looks paradoxical. Some organizations become open, participative, and socially responsible because their authoritarian leaders (most often their founders) are true believers in industrial democracy. These leaders use their authority to jump-start what they believe in—nonauthoritarian, people-oriented management. Instead of building autocratic organizations they build quasi-democratic ones, but by using quasi-authoritarian, top-down methods.

For example, the three founders of Saga Foods (where Abraham Maslow spent his later years)—"Hunk" Anderson, "Willie" Laughlin, and Bill Scandling—did just that. They had worked together as undergraduates to provide food service at Hobart College in upstate New York. When they graduated, the three decided to establish a company to do what they knew how to do: to provide quality food services for other colleges and universities. Their little start-up prospered, in part because they provided good food at fair prices but also because their company was, from its inception, people-centered. They had simply decided that Saga would operate in a humanistic way, and it did. They sought the counsel of many leading social scientists, Maslow among them, to help instill a humane, moral, and productive culture at their growing and, of course, hierarchical company.

In 1985, its final independent year, Saga's sales topped $1.25 billion, with profits of $29 million. In the very next year, 1986, Bill Scandling wrote the prophetic words, "The birds of prey have begun to circle."[6] Like many another effective middle-sized company, Saga disappeared that year, a tasty morsel snapped up by a much larger hierarchy.

The founders of many other companies did similar things, each in their own ways. Some, such as Saga, designed unique methods for weaving their own democratic, ethical values into the fabrics of their organizations. The CEOs of others, such as the Dana Corporation, used methods designed elsewhere. Dana introduced the Scanlon Plan, an early and effective union–management cooperation plan first developed in the 1950s by Joseph Scanlon, a United Steelworkers' officer.[7] The plan involves everyone in an organization, from CEO to maintenance staff, working in small groups to find ways to improve productivity. These improvements then result in immediate financial payoffs for everyone in the company. This idea so intrigued Professor Douglas McGregor that he induced Scanlon to come to MIT as a lecturer. From that bully pulpit, Scanlon was able to involve graduate students, local union leaders, and several CEOs to help him further develop and implement the plan.

Organizational leaders such as these authoritarian democrats can find themselves both burdened and blessed by their authority, burdened because authoritarianism sticks in their moral craws. They hold themselves, a bit like that grizzled Afghani chief of chapter 2, to be autonomous beings, neither other people's masters nor their servants, neither *in* control nor *under* control. Yet they are also blessed because they have achieved positions from which they can exercise much power and authority, and blessed, as well, because they can use that authority to limit authoritarianism in their organizations. They can use it to minimize the stifling effects of hierarchy and to augment the ennobling effects of something approaching industrial democracy. But through it all, they know, and their people know, that they can't quite go all the way.

When such quasi-democratized companies are realistic, when all concerned understand the *quasi* part of that compound word, their people will know that they must work hard, they must work long, and they must perform their share of unpleasant duties. They will also, however, be much less bugged by the underlying discomfort that besets many managers, a discomfort that derives from the coexisting and opposing pressures of decent humanism and hierarchical authoritarianism.

AUTHORITATIVE PRESENCE

Remember our story about Mike, the rookie manager who tried to use a participative style and then ran into trouble with the people upstairs? More seasoned managers probably wouldn't have gotten themselves into Mike's either-or trap. They would long since have understood that authority is the baseline, the sine qua non, of organizational life. Those managers therefore would have developed at least one part of a broad competency that one can call *authoritative presence*. The idea of authoritative presence can be loosely divided into two parts. Call them *authoritative savvy* and *authoritative aura*.

Authoritative Savvy

The savvy part includes an almost instinctive ability to take note, automatically and continuously, of the hierarchical aspects of the immediate organizational environs. It's as though managers with such presence must continuously, albeit only semiconsciously, be asking themselves questions like these: "Am I—right now—in the physical (or cyber) presence of my superiors, my peers, or my subordinates? Have I calibrated my words, posture, and tone of voice accordingly?" Such instrumental hierarchy-appropriate behavior is probably as nuanced as the countless fine adjustments any of us makes when driving on a busy freeway—and just as necessary for survival.

Some may not approve of this kind of behavior, regardless of its purpose. Especially in the Western world, we tend to take a dim view of such instrumentalism, considering it inauthentic, manipulative, and overly political. But it's not very different, is it, from similar social-instrumental behaviors that carry other more acceptable labels, such as "networking" or simply showing organizational common sense?[8] In many societies, moreover, getting things done through connections and personal relationships is simply the normal way to go. There, learning to be sensitive and responsive to formal—and informal—issues of rank, power, and family is a more central part of one's upbringing than it is in some other societies. We achievement-driven Westerners may profess to recoil from such exploitation of our personal relationships, even though most of us seem to do a certain amount of it. Does the moral test lie in the intent of such behavior? Is the behavior aimed primarily at self-aggrandizement or at helping to resolve significant organizational problems?

Effective manager/leaders comprehend such subtleties of hierarchical life. They know that they carry the blessing and burden of their own inescapable authority. They also know that they work within a larger authoritarian system. They know, too, that the realities of rank, power, and special personal relationships must inevitably distort communication and limit trust. More important, they learn to pinpoint where and when such distortions are most likely to occur, and what kinds of forces are most likely to generate bias and distrust.

So managers with authoritative savvy make continual adjustments in their dealings with the formal hierarchical system. They sense when to socialize with their people and when the time has come to stop socializing. They know when to keep pushing the boss and when the signals indicate it is time to stop pushing—for now. They are skilled in using authority without overusing it and in coping with higher authority exercised upon them.

Authoritative Aura

Managers who have such authoritative savvy are also likely to emanate, almost exude, another aspect of authoritative presence, an intangible aura of authority. They wear their authority comfortably and naturally. It takes years for some executives to reach this comfort level. Others show it from day one. They're naturals.

The rest of us are likely to sense an executive's authoritative aura quickly, albeit not always consciously. Indeed the authoritative presence of such practiced "hierarchists" usually shows up even when they're off duty. Some time ago, for example, my wife and I were invited to dinner at the home of a regional VP of a large, traditional, multinational company. He had this kind of authoritative presence, especially the aura part. It appeared almost immediately. During the meal he expressed considerable interest in a book we had recently written, *Hot Groups*.[9] "Just what is a 'hot group'?" he asked. "What evidence do you have that they work? What companies are using them? How do you put them together? They sound unruly and anarchistic. Can they be trusted to accomplish what you say they can?"

This perfectly reasonable battery of questions made us uncomfortable. They were asked politely enough, but they came from a place where he was and we weren't, from his fully internalized, authoritative home base. Was he overbearing? Domineering? Not at all. Can we write him off as just another autocratic bureaucrat? Far from it. He's a thoughtful, humane, and well-educated modern executive. But he is also steeped in the ways of hierarchy, so thoroughly infused with those ways, perhaps, that his on-the-job style extended even into off-the-job settings.

Managers who have authoritative aura don't necessarily also have authoritative savvy, and sometimes managers with savvy don't have much aura. Most of the time, though, these two aspects of broad authoritative presence hang together. Consider, for example, another experienced executive, the provost of a small, highly rated university who had just been selected to become president of a much larger one. She had both aspects of authoritative presence. She told me about her first encounter with a senior (male) administrator at her new location, someone who had expected that he himself should have been appointed in her stead. Now he would be reporting to her. He had initially been rather rude to her, she said. "He acted as though *he* were *my* boss. So I felt I had to set him straight, and that this was the right time to do it." Then this kindly, rather soft-spoken woman went on to explain how she had then and there made the lines of authority unmistakably clear. His choice, she had communicated to him, was either to accept her authority or to find another job. And she did it, I am sure, with the same authoritative presence that showed itself in our conversation. She fully understood, in depth, that basic reality of organizational life, the reality that human hierarchies require the exercise (and acceptance) of some degree of authority. That's the baseline—the bread of the managerial Dagwood sandwich.

The Downsides of Authoritative Presence

We should not leave this discussion without erecting a large DANGER sign. Authoritative presence can often run amok. Like other competencies, it can be pushed beyond reasonable limits. Authoritative aura can shade into inflated self-importance and autocratic, unilateral "leadership." And because some followers respond to such commanding authority, a circular dynamic can ensue. As people increasingly bow and scrape before them, executives can begin to believe that they truly are becoming kings of the hill. They then begin to assume more commanding postures. The cycle can soon cause simple authoritative aura to expand into delusions of omnipotence and godliness. When even great men and women begin to believe they are great, take cover!

Similarly, and perhaps even more often, authoritative savvy is also misused. Some managers have been known to develop so much savvy, that it takes over from the work itself. They spend their energy trying to develop buddy-buddy relationships with the "right" people, cozying up to those in power while putting down the people they see as competitors or enemies. Even in authoritarian hierarchies, fortunately, those sly foxes seldom make out very well over the long pull.

COUNTERPOINTS TO AUTHORITY: INFORMAL POWER STRUCTURES

New managers soon learn that hierarchical authority is not the only kind of power that they or others can muster. Every hierarchy's formal authority is paralleled by other informal sources of power, power that managers can use either to countervail against higher authority's excesses or to help the hierarchy get its work done. The power of numbers is one such source, as in the words of an old American trade union song: "The boss won't listen when one guy squawks, but he'd better listen when the union talks." The power of expertise is another, as when one of the chemists in the lab knows much more about a critical new product than anyone else in the world. Nor should we forget the powers of authoritative savvy, insider knowledge, and personal connections.[10]

Here are two examples of such informal power. As part of a larger study, I once interviewed a not very senior civil servant in the U.S. Department of Transportation. We were talking about the selection of staff for the new secretary of transportation. "Don't kid yourself," my interviewee said after we had chatted for a few minutes. "You probably think I'm just a flunky, but the truth is that I'm the one who makes the important personnel decisions around here. Secretaries of transportation come and go. They're just Christmas help. They don't have any idea of what's really going on. I'm the one who chooses the secretary's key people. Besides, I have lots of friends on the Hill."

I discovered later that many of this functionary's rather self-inflating assertions were true. By dint of his civil service status, his insider knowledge, and his "friends on the Hill," he did have a great deal of influence over who was selected for key jobs in DOT. His rank gave him little authoritative power, but he had amassed many other varieties.

Then there was the incident of the guy named Joe. Shortly after starting to work with the HR division of a large New England department store, I found myself scratching my head in puzzlement. Several times in meetings with senior staff, I would ask a question and someone would respond with, "Maybe we'd better ask Joe about that." Variants of that phrasing surfaced again and again: "What's Joe's opinion?" "Let's talk to Joe first." Finally I took one of the seniors aside and asked the obvious question: "Who the devil is this guy Joe? It seems everybody has to have his okay on every important decision." "Joe? Oh, Joe's the CEO's chauffeur. Officially he's part of this department, and occasionally he does a little filing and stuff like that. But mostly he's Mr. Robertson's driver." And she added, "He and Mr. Robertson have known one another for a very long time." Joe had little authority but plenty of another kind of power—connection power—that circumvented the hierarchy's authoritarian structure.

Every organization has all sorts of such informal sources of power. Several of these sources are closely related to what the preceding section called authoritative savvy. These kinds of power are most often found on the human side of the house, among real people with real faces and real personalities. These are people we may like or dislike, envy or compete with, people we talk to at water fountains and copy machines, and people on the other ends of e-mails.

Informal systems often serve to counter or subvert ideas and programs that the top of the hierarchy is trying to promote, but they can also serve organizationally supportive purposes. They can help to compensate for the formal system's communication failures. Indeed, the formal structure—and individual managers, too—would have a hard time getting their work done without the backup of those seldom-appreciated informal networks.

How Private Are "Private Secretaries"?

Organization charts may be pretty good indicators of formal authority, but they're terrible maps of informal power and real communication flows. Consider, for example, the organizational role that used to be called "private secretary." These days that job is more likely to get labels such as "executive assistant" or "personal aide"— but "private" remains the operational idea. Or perhaps even more appropriately (as my son pointed out in one of his novels), the word *secret* is embedded in the word *secretary*.

This special relationship between a boss and a close aide has been around in organizations for a long time. It almost always escapes hierarchical control. These secretaries, aides, and assistants all work for the organization, but most of them work even more for their immediate bosses. If a very senior executive were to question division director Sam Smith's secretary, Mary Jones, about her boss's activities, would we expect Ms. Jones to tell all? Wouldn't most of us expect her to do what then President Nixon's secretary did—back up her boss? We would expect her to show first loyalty to Smith and take a cautious stance about transmitting potentially hurtful information to anyone else.

These close secretaries are usually privy to their boss's particular idiosyncrasies and weaknesses, his or her anxieties, hopes, and disappointments. It is no accident that when the boss is promoted, the special assistant often moves up, too. The one is almost an extension of the other. The oft-told tales of male bosses and female secretaries (and now occasionally vice versa) becoming lovers are understandable, too. Theirs is likely to be a more personal, perhaps more intimate, relationship than any other in the organization.

Secretaries usually belong to different informal networks than their bosses, among them those made up of other secretaries. So they are likely to be excellent miners of the rich veins of rumor, gossip, and not yet public information that lie buried just beneath the surface of every large human organization. Nor are such informal channels necessarily harmful to the organizational hierarchy. On the contrary, dedicated and savvy managers use these back channels to help them do their jobs more expeditiously.

SOME PERSONAL DILEMMAS OF MIDDLE MANAGERIAL LIFE

Who, then, must balance humanistic values with the hierarchy's authoritarian realities? Who must be aware of organizational power in all its forms? Who must integrate conflicting humanizing and systemizing forces? Who else but middle managers—the men and women ensconced on the rungs between the bottoms and the tops of big organizations' hierarchical ladders. It takes experience, a sense of self-worth, savvy, and skill to balance on these rungs, to maintain one's personal integrity and humanity and still help the organization get serious work done.

It's the managers in the middle who can most easily become entangled in the integrity/authority/power net. For example, at an intensive off-site sensitivity training workshop, we once had five levels of management (all male) from the same company together in the same face-to-face group. There were several first-line supervisors—ex-blue-collar guys who had come up from the ranks—along with a couple of plant superintendents several higher-level department heads and on up to and including the CEO. The group had been arranged "diagonally," so as few direct reports as possible were in the same group. In a hierarchy, of course, it's impossible to follow that rule all the way up to the narrow top, so two VPs who reported directly to the CEO were in the group, too.

Initially, the group's agendaless discussion stayed cool and safe. The participants talked about easy-to-agree-on subjects: current business problems and suggestions for solving them. During that phase, everybody got into the act—the CEO, division directors, department heads, and, to a lesser extent, the first-line supervisors. Gradually, though, the talk turned to touchier issues: recurrent foulups, alleged mistreatment of people, and cover-ups of serious managerial mistakes. As these more sensitive topics entered the discussion, the decibel level decreased. Those just below the CEO were among the first to drop into near silence, followed by the next level down and so on, until the meeting became pretty much a two-way talkfest, with first-line supervisors laying it on the line and the CEO responding. The others, sandwiched between the two ends, sat mostly silent, almost frozen in their seats.

I had a chance to talk with the CEO just after the session. He was delighted with the whole thing. He said something like this: "Did you notice how easily those first-line supers and I could communicate with each other? They're the salt of the earth. They're not afraid to say what they think. Those other guys, they're technical types, intellectuals. They cover their tails. That's why they shut up. If we're going to build a solid top-to-bottom team around here, they're the ones who need the real work."

Was the CEO reading the situation correctly? I had to tell him I didn't think so. But he was certainly right about one thing. Those middle levels, especially the upper middles, *were* covering their tails—for good reason. I thought the middle folks had shut up because they were just plain scared by the presence of their close bosses, especially the CEO. If the in-betweens had argued with first-line supervisors, they would probably have been called to the boss's office the next morning. The first-line supervisors, however, didn't need to feel afraid. The CEO was too distant, too far up the hierarchy to scare them. The chief executive of a large organization wasn't likely to go after a veteran foreman, four levels down the hierarchy. Besides, if these old-timers pointed to things that were going wrong, who was likely to be held responsible? Certainly not the top boss! That was middle managers' territory.

As for the CEO, he was feeling heroic. He had shown himself to be one of the good old boys, duking it out with the real working folks. It was fun, like doffing his suit and tie and climbing into a gray (not pink!) jumpsuit—for one afternoon. But for those in between, saying the wrong thing could easily have turned into a CLS—a career-limiting statement.

The meeting must have been stressful for the middle managers. It spotlighted and dramatized that classic hierarchical dilemma— the dilemma of dependency—and some of the difficulties involved in speaking truth to power.

On Speaking Truth to Power

In a scene from Sophocles' *Antigone*, a sentry carries bad news to King Creon. The king is infuriated by what he hears and blames the sentry, who barely escapes with his life. Once safely out of Creon's presence, the terrified sentry mutters: "[O]ne thing's for sure: You won't catch me coming back again. It's a goddam miracle I got out of 'ere alive."[11]

Surely that sentry's plight resonates with many of us. Carrying bad news to powerful people can be dangerous. Indeed, it takes courage to disagree even modestly with those in authority. For most of us, though, and most of the time, saying what we think is not a central issue in our day-to-day working lives. It's an issue that flares up only once in a while, when some unusual challenge arises. Yet, rare though they may be, such events are likely to be critical points in the lives of hierarchies' middle managers. That's when those CLSs so often happen. Organizations have long memories, so even one or two such mistakes can have long-term effects.

When we find ourselves asking, "Do I dare say what I think?" too frequently, many of us are driven to make a choice: We must either speak the truth as we see it—and face the consequences—or modify our positions and perhaps rationalize until we believe that ours are the views that need adjustment. That's bad enough when the issues in question relate to things external to our basic values, such as marketing policies or manufacturing processes. But when our core beliefs are on the line, when our sense of honesty and integrity begins to nag at us, "adjustment" becomes personally costly and painful. Yet, if we fail to raise our voices at such moments, we become colluders in the erosion of our own moral fabric.

Examples, unfortunately, continue to be easy to find, even twenty-four centuries after Sophocles' play. Here's one from today's Wall Street Journal:

> *In 1996, [Ms. Betty Vinson] took a job as a midlevel accountant at a small long-distance company. Five years later, her solid career took a sudden turn in a very sorry direction. Today Ms. Vinson, 47 years old, is awaiting sentencing on conspiracy and securities-fraud charges. . . .*
>
> *The long-distance company grew up to be telecom giant World-Com Inc., which melted down last year in an $11 billion fraud, the biggest in corporate history. . . . Asked by her bosses there to make false accounting entries, Ms. Vinson balked—and then caved. Over the course of six quarters she continued to make the illegal entries to bolster WorldCom's profits at the request of her superiors. Each time she worried. Each time she hoped it was the last time. . . . Ms. Vinson's story is a cautionary tale. . . . When an employee's livelihood is on the line, it's tough to say no to a powerful boss. Ms. Vinson wasn't alone in these predicaments. In a report issued this month, investigators hired by the company's new board found that dozens of employees knew about the fraud at WorldCom but were afraid to speak out.*[12]

Authoritarian hierarchies are good at playing that devil's game. Once inside hierarchy's walls, we may too easily be caught up in our institution's all-consuming social surroundings. We can begin to feel that our organizational world is the whole world. Hierarchies are great at seducing us into reshaping our reality into their reality. They can entice managers away from their authenticity with bonuses, golden parachutes, and the most seductive inducement of all, power. They can dress up avarice so that it's almost indistinguishable from generosity, and they can make cruelty look like kindness. Once managers are embedded in such environments, their integrity can easily evaporate.

It takes savvy and ego strength for a manager, especially a novice, to cope with hierarchies' siren songs. Some can't do it. They give in.

They sacrifice their integrity to become feeble pawns of their hierarchies' wills. Others won't do it. They get out. They break away to find another way of life. Many, though, do thread their way through the moral maze. Some find it fairly easy because they are lucky enough to work in organizations that have high ethical standards. Others develop enough self-esteem and authoritative presence to cope with even the most tempting organizational carrots and the most threatening organizational sticks.

In recent years, the dilemma has become a trilemma. Managers can no longer safely count on guarantees from the organization's side. No matter how exemplary their performance or how loyal they may be, Mother Company may still abandon them, with little notice and often little remorse. So job insecurity has been added to the mix. Give in to the authority of the organization? Hold out for your own sense of what's right? Hope that your choices will help you hang on to your uncertain job?

In big hierarchies, the middle managerial highway is pitted with such psychological potholes. Despite valiant humanizing efforts, it will continue that way. Traveling that road requires a fine, continuous interplay among a triangle of forces: one's personal values, the real (not the professed) standards of the organization, and the need to keep the family's refrigerator full.

Fortunately, managers rarely find themselves forced to make a clean choice among these options. Most of the time it isn't a matter of standing up for one's beliefs or kowtowing to malevolent authority or just doing whatever it takes to keep one's job—although, as some whistle-blowers will attest, it can certainly come to that. Mostly managers live in a kind of middle world. With some notable exceptions, big hierarchies usually try to operate close to the moral standards we all share. They also try to reward loyalty. And managers, for their part, try—carefully—to communicate truth to upstairs power as well as to the downstairs people who depend on them. Managing is no longer the rough, tough, macho game it is still often pictured to be. It has become a delicate, sometimes dangerous, often subtle relational dance, perhaps more akin to courtship than to rugby.

IN SUMMARY

Hierarchies aren't what they used to be. They've been somewhat flattened, networked, and teamed. Nor is authority what it used to be. It has been softened, even cloaked in cordiality. But it's still there, and it's still the central reality of organizational life.

The novice manager had better not believe that the new has actually replaced the old. It hasn't. Hierarchy and its ever-faithful sidekick, authority, still call the tune. Although a fog of modernism may obscure them, both remain lively and vigorous. These twins continue to cause managers headaches and heartaches, but they also continue to get big things done. Although most of us don't like authoritarianism, we do like that other part, getting things done. That has led to a kind of tacit agreement among all concerned, an agreement to act as though our big, hierarchical organizations are much more consistent with our democratic values than they really are.

Managers get caught in the resultant squeeze. Humanizing forces in the organization teach new managers to behave participatively, downplaying or even denying their authority. But authority is managers' medium, the air they breathe. With experience, managers learn, like it or not, that they are their employees' boss and their boss's employee. They learn to use their authority, but only rarely, leaving it locked up most of the time, out of sight although never out of mind. Some managers—probably the most effective ones—develop authoritative presence, an almost instinctive ability to deal with their hierarchical surroundings and to develop a comfortable relationship with their own authority. They communicate that presence so that others quickly sense it. They understand that authority is a decisive determinant of their managerial fates, but they also understand that authority isn't nearly the whole of it. They learn to use the many informal varieties of power and influence that hide in every nook and cranny of human hierarchies. They learn such things, and then they must try to make them fit with their personal standards of morality and integrity—and *not* the other way round.

Perhaps it's largely because of the complexities and conundrums facing managers in our new world of knowledge and technology that leadership has become a pervasive topic. Authority, the tool that hierarchical organizations lend to their managers, may have been adequate when authoritarian hierarchies were simple top-down, command-and-control systems. They're no longer that way. They're cross-connected, fast-changing, and full of contradictory pressures.

So maybe managers can no longer be simply managers. Maybe, to deal with the complications of the new organizational world, dull old managers must become shiny new leaders—or must they? Does anybody know what a real leader is? Do managers still need authority to lead, or does their authority just get in the way? Or is all the current talk about leadership just another way of loading even more on the middle manager's already burdened back? These are some of the questions chapter 7 tries to answer.

SEVEN

Leadership, Authority, and the Hierarchy

We're hooked on leaders! Especially over the past twenty or so years, Western organizations and educational institutions have become so enamored, even infatuated, with the concept of leadership that no B-school would dare omit a goodly serving of leadership courses from its curriculum. Yet most of these courses weren't around twenty years ago. What's changed? Are we in more desperate need of competent leaders? One hypothesis: Our enormously increased attention to leadership may be an acceptable (albeit devious) way for those who dislike hierarchies to acknowledge that hierarchies aren't dead. For where there are leaders there are almost always followers. Where there are leaders cum followers, there is also hierarchy.

Here is another, perhaps more useful, hypothesis: Organizations are still hierarchies, but they've changed. They've gone participative and analytic and groupy, all at the same time. These and other pieces of the new organizational jigsaw puzzle don't always fit together, but middle managers still must try to integrate them. To do that, therefore, let's convert *managers* with authority into *leaders* with the charisma, persuasiveness, and vision they need to get this difficult task done.

For those and other reasons, organizations have been changing in major ways, flattening and opening up their hierarchies. In the face of these changes, the qualities associated with leadership—qualities such as vision and a sense of purpose—can no longer be reserved to the few at the pinnacles of great hierarchies, to CEOs such as Jack Welch, Steve Jobs, or Lou Gerstner. More than ever, organizations will need those qualities from managers at all levels. Hence the current push away from managing, toward leading. Organizations are trying to move leadership downward to managers on lower and still lower rungs of the hierarchical ladder. Perhaps that's the main idea behind the enormous amount of work being done to find ways to teach and train leaders, to research the nature of leadership, and to instill more of the qualities of leaders into managers.

This chapter is about that shift from treating middle managing as mostly managing to treating it as mostly leading. Just what does that change involve? Can companies send plain middle managers off to leadership development seminars for extreme makeovers and have them come back as bright new leaders? And if the conversion succeeds, will a hierarchy of leaders help solve modern organizations' major problems?

We can begin by trying to clarify the concept of leadership. What, exactly, is leadership? If you're now a manager, would you like to become a leader *instead of* a manager? Or *as well as* a manager? What are the differences, if any, between the two? What are the qualities one would have to develop to become a "real" leader? And finally, this chapter raises some possible consequences of organizations populated by leaders instead of managers.

WHAT'S A LEADER?

Answering this question isn't easy. The territory called *leadership* is a quagmire. Over the years, but especially over the past decade, dozens of leadership institutes, leadership training centers, leadership departments in B-schools, and leadership research units have opened their doors to students and executives. In mid-2004, the four-volume, 2,120 page *Encyclopedia of Leadership* was published.[1]

Amazon.com today lists more than 70,000 books about leadership. Add to these the thousands and more thousands of scholarly and not so scholarly papers on the topic. Everyone and her brother is ready to tell us definitively what leadership really is, who the greatest leaders—emperors, prime ministers, generals, and CEOs—really were or are, and how those great leaders got that way, even though most of the people usually cited got there by unique and irreproducible pathways.

The humorist Dave Barry caught the flavor of the obscurity and ambiguity surrounding the notion of leadership in a column announcing that he had decided to run for president. He feels he should do it because our nation needs "leadership." So his campaign theme will be "A leader who will lead by leading."[2] Sometimes, as one peruses the leadership literature, Barry's vacuous phrasing looks right on. The idea of leadership is so broad and unbounded, and the definitions so varied, that humanizers, systemizers, and everyone else can find pieces to fit any preconceptions.

True blue, all-out humanizers, for example, like the whole idea of leadership, and they are eager to convert managers to the leadership creed. They've had enough of managers. In their view, managing is a hierarchical notion, born of the organization chart. Managers are people who do what their job descriptions specify. But leaders, for humanizers, are their own men and women, independent, autonomous, and beholden to no one, much like the Afghani chieftain in the Kipling story back in chapter 2. Systemizers, however, still want their managers to carry on as managers, to go right on working by the book and getting their projects done on schedule and within budget. For reasons of the speeding, complicated, and uncertain new world, though, they would also like to inject a small dose of leadership elixir into most managers.

So this chapter can promise neither a neat, unambiguous definition of a leader nor a list of the seven magic secrets that will make you one. Yet, messy as it is, the concept of leadership cannot be sloughed off. It is important for contemporary managers. It's important because managers need other tools besides their formal authority to do well in modern organizations. They have always needed other tools, of course, such as interpersonal skills and expertise at relevant tasks. Now they need those and still other tools more than ever. The fabled land of leadership may be a good place to search for some of those tools.

How Can You Know One When You Meet One?

Leadership is a hard concept to pin down, in part because many kinds of human beings have been squeezed into the same boat, all labeled *leaders*. What's a leader? How about an inspirational wartime master of rhetoric, like Winston Churchill, or an indirect leader who breaks open new pathways, like Albert Einstein, or a charismatic preacher like the Reverend Billy Graham, or a low-key, dedicated soul like Mother Teresa? What about a visionary like Martin Luther King, Jr., or a fighter for human rights like Susan B. Anthony, or a power-driven self-server like Saddam Hussein, or a steadfast, committed figure like Nelson Mandela? Then there are the leaders who look pretty bad until they step forward to take charge in times of crisis, like Mayor Rudy Giuliani of New York on 9/11/01. And let's not forget those we hail as leaders because they build successful organizations, like yesterday's Alfred P. Sloan at GM or Jack Welch at GE. Nor can we ignore leaders who ride their organizations into destruction, like Ken Lay at Enron. All these different kinds of people, and countless others, are widely referred to as leaders.

Three Themes: Transformation, Persuasion, Competence

With all these goings-on, it's hard to locate the core of the leadership apple. Is there really any *there* there? Are there any basics common to all or most of the diverse set of people we call leaders? Yes. If one sifts through and culls the myriad definitions and descriptions, at least three underlying themes recur.

Theme 1: Leading is about *transforming*. James MacGregor Burns first talked about transforming leaders in 1978.[3] The idea caught on because many observers agreed that some leaders (by implication, the admirable ones) are visionaries who effect significant changes (by implication, positive changes) in their sectors of the world.

Theme 2: Leading is about *persuading*, about being able to influence other people to do or believe what leaders want them to do or believe. John Gardner, a wise, competent, and humanizing leader, put that idea straightforwardly: "Leadership is the process of persuasion (or example) by which an individual (or leadership team) induces a group to pursue objectives held by the leader or shared by the leader and his or her followers."[4] That's a useful, if not perfectly precise, definition.

Theme 3 comes from my old mentor, MIT's Doug McGregor, another wise and widely experienced humanizing leader. He used to say that leaders are people who communicate two things to their followers: competence and confidence, an idea that captures much of what I have called authoritative presence. Indeed, it's via these two qualities that leaders acquire followers. If I feel that someone is competent to do the job that he and the rest of us are undertaking, and if he also makes me feel confident that he has my interests at heart, he can probably persuade me to follow, and therefore qualifies to be called a leader.

COMPLICATIONS OF LEADERSHIP

Unfortunately, a variety of side issues further complicates the already complicated concept of leadership. If you are trying to decide whether you want to become a leader and whether you could become one if you tried, you should be aware of these complications. Don't walk too casually into the leadership minefield.

What About Bad Leaders?

All three of the leadership themes—transformation, persuasion, and competence and confidence—carry a positive tone. Leaders, by implication, are good people. But there is surely no shortage of bad people who are also effective transformers and persuaders and who are undeniably competent. Do these edifying definitions of leaders rule out such people? Was Adolph Hitler not a leader? How about Osama bin Laden? Jim Jones of Jonestown? Chainsaw Al Dunlap of Sunbeam?

Do such individuals belong in another category? They have certainly influenced many people. Do we label them despots or charlatans or con men and women, but not leaders? Even though thousands of committed followers cheered many of them on and even willingly gave up their lives for some of them? In Jonestown, the number of men, women, and children who were persuaded to kill themselves at Jones's exhortation exceeded nine hundred! Perhaps he was not the kind of leader you may want to become, but was he not a leader?

Followers Can Create Leaders

We humans don't simply follow our current leaders. To alleviate our own anxieties, we often work very hard to create new ones. It's the dependency issue again. Especially in times of crisis, Jean Lipman-Blumen points out, we are wont to seek, even to demand, strong, take-charge figures who will promise us safety from the dangers that beset us.[5] Under such conditions, even those who know they cannot fulfill such superhuman requirements may feel that they must act as though they can. To still our terror, they try to maintain the illusion that they have the power to protect us. Mommy must sit by our bed and behave as though she can really guard us against the fearsome noises of the night. We press our physician to reassure us that everything will be all right, even when he is quite unsure. And if our physician is thrust repeatedly into that omnipotent role, she may come to believe she actually has such powers.

So we don't just follow our leaders. We anxious and dependent followers often set them up via a process that can generate at least two kinds of toxic monsters: leaders who leap at the chance to play godlike roles, and leaders who eventually—because their followers keep kowtowing before them—come to believe that they really have the powers their anxious and needy followers want to ascribe to them. Don't get caught up in that dangerous game.

Humans Are Superb Cognitive Balancers

There's plenty of evidence from social psychology to show that we humans don't just do what we believe. We also believe what we do.[6]

Attitudes influence behavior, but behavior also influences attitudes. If a leader—a boss or a preacher or a salesperson—can pressure or con you into doing just a little bit of something you feel is wrong, there's a good chance that you will then go on to seduce yourself into thinking it was actually an OK thing to do. Then you may rationalize your way into doing more of it. It couldn't really be very bad, could it? Otherwise why would a good person like you be doing even a little of it?

That process is so common that it even has names. Sometimes it's called the *foot in the door* phenomenon or, more conceptually, *cognitive balancing*. The underlying process is probably well understood, whatever its name, by most despots, con artists, and door-to-door salespeople. Moreover, if the people urging us on are leaders—glamorous and powerful role models—the whole change process becomes much easier. That's what seems to have happened to some naïve people caught up in a major financial scandal at Richard Scrushy's HealthSouth Corporation.[7] Many young men and women from small towns in the southeastern United States went to work for Health-South, attracted, it appears, by the nearly irresistible glamor, wealth, and chance to do social good that the company promised. Who would resist such an attractive opportunity? Some of the things they were later asked to do probably didn't feel quite right, but if these rich, powerful, sophisticated leaders were doing them, then maybe doing just a little of the same couldn't really be too bad. And when one has done a little, doing more is easier. So *en garde!* If leaders with more authority than you try to get the wrong foot in your door, slam it.

These two processes—the positive, leadership-type persuasion that most of us like, and the power-manipulative and authoritarian kinds of persuasion that we don't like—aren't psychologically far apart.

Doesn't Authority Make Leaders of Us All?

There is a psychological connection between formal authority and the concept of leadership, a connection that should not be overlooked. When your organization's hierarchy dubs you with authority, middle manager, you feel it. It changes you. You know that you have been given something special, some power you didn't have before and also some personal responsibility. The fact of our authority almost forces us to feel like something of a leader, to behave the way we think a leader should behave. Perhaps, thereby, it can even help us to become a leader.

Here's a small personal example. It happened a long, long time ago, but I still remember it very well. So it must not have been as trivial for me as it may now sound:

I had just the day before been commissioned an ensign in the U.S. Naval Reserve. I was twenty-one and I had received zero training. (Well, not quite zero. I had been shown how to salute and instructed not to shake hands with enlisted personnel.) Decked out for the first time in my brand new uniform, I was heading south from Boston on a train bound for my first duty station. My rail car was packed with soldiers, sailors, and marines, along with several civilians. After a couple of dull, smoky hours, a fistfight suddenly broke out between a sailor and a marine. Things began to get rough. I looked around. There were no other officers in that car. Then I looked down at my brand new single gold stripe. It signaled, I felt, that I was the person who was required to act. That stripe— and not my vision or charisma or personal persuasiveness—meant that it was my responsibility to stop the fight. So, somewhat tremulously, I got up and ordered those two big guys to break it up. And, by golly, they saw my stripe, and they obeyed. The fighting stopped.

Was that leadership or not? It apparently influenced the fighters, but more important, it influenced *me.* That stripe of authority made me do it, made me feel a responsibility I would certainly not have felt without it. In the current jargon, we would probably say that my single gold stripe of authority "empowered" me.

Gardner surely didn't mean to include that kind of exercise of authority when he wrote about leadership and persuasion. He probably would have called what I did coercion, not persuasion. Gardner meant persuasion in a more positive sense: persuasion by turning people on to new possibilities, much like Burns's notion of transformation. Yet authority can certainly be persuasive, and it can make its bearer feel persuasive, too. It can make one, even force one, to take initiatives. Isn't that a form of leadership?

Be careful. It's easy to interpret your formal authority—something loaned to you by your hierarchical organization—as though it were personal leadership, something with which you are specially endowed. It's easy to fall into that trap. We often refer to people as leaders because of their rank, regardless of their personal qualities. We call the president of the United States our leader—any president, no matter how unpersuasive or poor an exemplar. We call second lieutenants in the military platoon leaders even if their platoon members think their leader doesn't know his sidearm from a hole in the ground. The North Koreans refer to their rather strange president, Kim Chong-Il, not only as their leader but also as The Great Leader. Burns, however, and perhaps Gardner, probably wouldn't count these people as leaders, not unless they influenced their followers primarily by non-authoritarian forms of persuasion. All of this further fogs the concept of leadership.

Implicit Expectations

A colleague of mine used to say that he didn't understand all the fuss we humanizers make about developing fancy ways of persuading people who work for us to do what we want them to do. The best way, he argued, is simply to ask them. "Henry, will you please do X?" Ninety percent of the time, my friend asserted, Henry will do X and do it without complaint and without resentment. He will do it in part because he has been reared to believe that people should try to help one another. But most of the reason Henry will do it is that he knows you're his boss, and he *expects* to obey such requests from his boss. It's what bosses have a legitimate right to ask. It's all part of the implicit contract between Henry and the organization that hired him.

I think my colleague was right. Over a broad range, our expectations govern much of our behavior. It's that last 10 percent that's difficult. It's when our expectations are violated that we are most likely to resist or fight back—or when we are asked to change our behavior in ways important to our psyches, or when the boss demands that we do something we believe is morally wrong or detrimental to our organization.

Your subordinates, then—or, if you're a leader, your followers—carry expectations about your legitimate authority. As long as you stay within the bounds of their expectations, the mere fact of your authority will help you get many things done. It's when you want to break out of the usual bounds that your leadership skills—persuasiveness, inspiration, and all the rest—really come into play. Because breaking bounds is now part of everyday organizational life, it's a good reason for a manager to develop those 10 percent leadership skills.

Adding It All Up

You may feel somewhat irritated at this point. Perhaps you're thinking something like this: Whoa! Stop right there! Either I'm befuddled, or you are. First, you give me Burns. He says leaders are people who transform the world. Then Gardner, who says it's all a matter of persuasion. Then you tack on McGregor. He says leaders are people whose followers think their leaders are competent and take their followers' welfare seriously. And, incidentally, you've only mentioned the people on the receiving end of leadership once or twice, and not until late in the game. And when you do, you say followers create leaders, not the other way round. Don't leaders "create" followers?

Then you tell me that 90 percent of leadership is unnecessary. That people in organizations don't need to be led. They expect to do their jobs. And you imply that my managerial authority won't help much if I want to become a leader, although its implicit presence is what makes my people do most of what I ask. And it also makes me feel a leadership kind of responsibility. Besides, almost all the leaders you mentioned a few paragraphs ago—Welch, Churchill, Kim Chong-Il—had plenty of authority, and if they hadn't, I doubt that they'd be remembered as leaders.

I know that being a leader isn't *just* about authority. It has to do with vision, skill, integrity, expertise, charisma, and more. Some of the best leaders aren't even in hierarchies. They don't have *any* hierarchical authority. They just have the right stuff, and that makes people willing to follow them. But are you telling me, a manager in a hierarchy, that I should dump my authority if I want to become a real leader? And even if I wanted to, how could I? Just one chapter back you told me the company has tattooed it on me. This is all really confusing.

I warned you that this area was a morass. I don't exactly like the leadership-without-authority angle either, especially given that people with authority and the power attached to it have "persuaded" many people to do lots of pretty bad things in lots of situations over lots of years. Perhaps that's not *real* leadership, but it's been very persuasive, and its practitioners have transformed many companies, communities, and nations. Moreover, almost everyone refers to such people as leaders.

Maybe there's a way out, although this one may irritate you even more. Maybe authority—like my ensign's stripe on that train—gives only the *appearance* of persuasion. Authoritarian leaders such as Saddam and Stalin got people to act the way they wanted them to, but that doesn't mean that those people *believed* what they were preaching. Superficial obedience to authority certainly isn't the same as real commitment. Organizations have a surfeit of yes-men and yes-women who smile and agree with their bosses but don't really buy into a word of it. If you want belief, commitment, and those other good things, it takes real leadership—vision, integrity, and maybe charisma—to get you there. Authoritarian power alone won't do it.

That may sound great, but now I have to negate much of what I just wrote. How about the cognitive balancing act outlined a few paragraphs ago? If the conditions are right, authoritative power *will* generate commitment. If I can get you to do it, you may begin to believe it! That happened again and again to American prisoners during the Korean war.[8]

Of course, these other qualities of leadership—such as General Patton's and General DeGaulle's in WWII—don't automatically come along with authority. These qualities, as you said, are attached to special, unusual individuals, who, by nature or experience, really have the right stuff. But if Patton or DeGaulle hadn't held his authoritative rank, could he have been the same leader? Was his rank irrelevant to his leadership? Could he really have inspired his troops without the help of his stars?

The concept of leadership, it's worth repeating, is very popular, but it's not very clear. Yet, whatever it may be called, organizations need more of it from their managers, more than what authority by itself can provide.

Organizations Own Your Authority but Not Your Leadership Skills

Hierarchical organizations aren't necessarily *against* other forms of persuasion; it's just that—from the organization's point of view— authority is an instrument that has many advantages. For one thing, formal authority is owned by the organization and is only lent to the manager. The organization can tattoo bits of it on anyone and, if necessary, later add to or remove the tattoos. Formal hierarchical authority is thus quite independent of the personal qualities of the people who get it. The organization can anoint any damn fool with enough authority to become at least moderately influential. That's what my ensign's stripe did for and to me.

Leadership, however, isn't like that. It's not something organizations can give to their managers and then take away. The qualities of leadership belong to the person not to the organization. Organizations can certainly help by setting up conditions that encourage the development of managerial leaders, but even if they succeed, they won't own the products. Each individual manager will own them.

More leadership thus suggests greater diversity in organizations, less standardization. It suggests the need for managerial leaders in large numbers, each with a unique vision and aspiration. Can organizations tolerate that much diversity?

MANAGERS AND LEADERS: WHAT'S THE DIFFERENCE?

With everything now perfectly clear, let's go on just a little longer. The "What's a real leader?" issue becomes even more clouded by the propensity of many writers (especially humanizing writers, myself sometimes included) to take a *normative* stance, to equate real leaders with good guys, people with pockets full of stellar qualities. Somehow, being a leader comes out looking great, whereas being a manager is OK but nothing special. Positive words such as *integrity*, *vision*, and *inspiration* are sprinkled like fairy dust through contemporary writings on leadership, but managership doesn't get anything like that kind of panache.

Researchers who have studied differences between managers and leaders tend to go in that direction. They put white hats on leaders and gray to black ones on managers. In 1977, for example, Abraham Zaleznik published a classic piece called "Managers and Leaders: Are They Different?" "A manager," he wrote, "is a problem solver . . . Managers tend to adopt impersonal, if not passive, attitudes toward goals . . . Leaders work . . . to develop fresh approaches . . . to open issues for new options." And elsewhere, in the same article, he writes, "Managers relate to people according to the role they play . . . while leaders, concerned with ideas, relate in more intuitive and empathetic ways." Zaleznik goes on to characterize managers as more focused on getting work done, whereas leaders are more visionary, looking toward long-term possibilities.[9] Which of the two sounds more attractive—manager or leader?

Since then, other writers trying to delineate differences between managers and leaders have arrived at even sharper, more definitive contrasts. Warren Bennis, in his 2003 revision of *On Becoming a Leader*, succinctly and lucidly details a list of such differences, a list that more or less fits with Burns's idea of transforming leaders and also parallels what Zaleznik observed. Here are a few of Bennis's contrasts:

> *The manager administers; the leader innovates.*
> *The manager maintains; the leader develops.*
> *The manager focuses on systems and structure; the leader*
>   *focuses on people.*
> *The manager relies on control; the leader inspires trust.*
> *The manager asks how and when; the leader asks what and why.*
> *The manager has his or her eye on the bottom line; the leader's*
>   *eye is on the horizon.*
> *The manager does things right; the leader does the right things.*[10]

One can't help noticing how regularly the comparisons between managers and leaders come down on the same side—the leaders' side. Somehow leaders always look bigger and better than plain vanilla managers. Everyone seems to want to make leaders out of managers, not managers out of leaders. Managers are earthbound and ordinary. Leaders reach for the stars.

That's partly because "manager" is a job title—only a name that can be tagged on to anybody, like "salesclerk." But to become a leader, one must embark on a great life journey. Effective leadership must come from within the person. It can't be granted by the organization. A manager is someone who has been appointed to a job. A leader, as described in much of the literature, is a great human being, a paragon, the person every mother's child should aspire to become.

If that's so, then let's help everyone become a leader! And that, incidentally, is what many people are trying to do—by introducing leadership courses into high schools, leadership programs into communities, and many, many leadership workshops into business organizations. Why not? If leaders are synonymous with fine human beings, then the more the better.

But let's also acknowledge what we're doing. If we all become leaders, where will we find followers? It begins to sound like the story that used to be told about the department of Egyptology at the University of Chicago. Not very many students chose to major in that field, so the several professors had to compete, the story went, to see which one would get the student.

Even Systemizers Want a Touch of Leadership

If leaders have such glorious attributes, who needs prosaic old managers? Systemizers do, even though they're now also looking with more favor upon leaders. They want managers who will get the basics done on time and right, who will make sure that the organizational engine is properly tuned, who will move the product off the loading dock, and who will, in fact, keep at least one eye on the bottom line. These days they want leaders, too, with their other eye on the horizon, but even more they want managers, with both feet on solid ground.

How come hard-headed systemizers no longer, as they once did, view all the noise about leadership as soft-headed fluff? There are at least three reasons: First, the volatile, fast-moving, interconnected world has driven them to modify their stance. Even the dourest systemizer will surely admit that today's organizations require some reasonable amount of leaderlike creativity and spontaneity from all levels of the organization—as long as that kind of behavior doesn't take managers outside the bounds of discipline and good order.

Second, the environment is not the only thing that has changed. Organizations' top executives (I dare not call them organizations' leaders) have changed, too. They come from a newer generation. They move faster. They look with more favor on imagination and inspiration. They recognize that their managers are people, not empty suits. They want, at least up to a point, managers who have the positive qualities of leadership.

And a third reason: Managers no longer work only within their own units. They must interact with all sorts of others, with diverse customers, and with people from other cultures and nations as well as other groups in their own organizational hierarchy. Even lower-level managers need to be able to persuade horizontally and diagonally, to envision the big picture, and to relate to all the changes going on out there.

FROM MANAGERS TO LEADERS

Notice that none of our three themes of leadership says much about the central topic of the preceding chapter, managers' authority. Leadership is about transformation and persuasion and so on, but isn't authority also a tool for transforming organizations and persuading people? That's certainly why organizations dole out different rations of it to managers at different hierarchical levels. They do it to make sure that their people don't take the U.S. Declaration of Independence too seriously—at least the line about all men being created equal. They distribute authority in different quantities to ensure that managers at different levels will be quite *un*equal. They want the people who have more authority to be able to persuade those with less—not only via what Burns or Gardner would call leadership but also via the fallback of authoritative power. And they do all that because by controlling the distribution of authority they also control the organization's structure, its discipline and orderliness.

An organization full of leaders is likely to be much harder to control, let alone standardize, than an organization full of managers. That's because leadership isn't a commodity. The qualities of leadership, it's worth repeating, aren't transferable. Each individual leader is thus likely to be quite different from every other, each his or her own person. That's probably why many big hierarchical organizations were reluctant, until recently, to encourage very many of their people to go the leadership route. They would rather save that for the few near the top.

Now, however, massive complexity, brought on by technological and social change, is making organizations look differently at leadership and at the diversity that accompanies it. It's my guess that traditional hierarchical forces will sooner or later clash with liberalizing leadership forces, that another battle between humanizers and modern, somewhat liberalized systemizers lies ahead of us. The reason? Humanizers will push the idea of converting managers to leaders. If they succeed too well, counterforces will be generated. Eventually, these forces will push back toward more managing and less leading, toward more uniformity and less diversity.

Until then, in big hierarchical organizations, the leadership idea will probably ride high. And while it does, middle managers would be well advised to take advantage of it. All this interest in leadership gives managers a chance to reassert their individuality and to ponder such oft-neglected questions as these: Who am I? What do I believe is really important? What do I believe is right? The relentlessly pressing, almost frenetic character of managerial life too often drives such questions far to the backs of our minds.

IS THE FOCUS ON LEADERSHIP AN INDIRECT ACKNOWLEDGMENT OF HIERARCHY?

Humanizers want more leaders in organizations. That's a giant step toward more diversity. Isn't it also a giant step toward acknowledging the hierarchy? Leaders imply followers (many humanizers prefer the more active word *constituents*), and leaders-plus-followers means hierarchy—not the old rigid hierarchy, to be sure, but hierarchy nonetheless. This time around, many dedicated humanizers are perhaps not thinking so much about getting rid of hierarchies as about infiltrating them with persuasive, modern leaders—people who know themselves and can relate to others with much more than just their hierarchical authority.

Moreover, when hard-headed systemizers begin to talk leadership, they are no longer busily standardizing and routinizing everything and everyone. They're backing off enough to think instead about the need of modern organizations for diverse and gifted individuals—motivators, innovators, visionaries. They are looking for alternative ways to inject leadership qualities into their hierarchies' managers. So in the short run, we may be approaching a temporary cease-fire between the two, with humanizers showing some tolerance for hierarchies and systemizers making room for the variability that must accompany the focus on leadership.

All in all, the current concerns of big organizations and scholars about leadership can thus be interpreted as both an acknowledgment of the hierarchy and a simultaneous awareness that there's more to modern managing than hierarchy alone can handle. The uniform, impersonal methods that pure systemizers understand, such as the use of authority and rank, can't keep the new multi-ring circus running. But the fact that hierarchical authority is no longer sufficient doesn't mean it is no longer necessary.

IN SUMMARY

Leadership has become the most widely discussed, widely taught, and widely written about subject in the world of organizational studies. It may also be one of the foggiest. At least three common denominators partially bind this inchoate realm together: Leaders are individuals who are able to transform relevant aspects of other peoples' worlds, who can successfully persuade others to change their behavior, and who can gain others' confidence in them and in their competence.

Both humanizers and systemizers seem to like parts of this broad, loosely bounded concept of leadership. Humanizers want managers to convert to the leadership faith because leaders influence in humanistic ways—via vision, sensitivity, personal charisma, and commitment to a superordinate purpose. Systemizers still like down-to-earth managers who get the job done, but now they seem willing to go for a little leading as well.

Middle managers find themselves in a curious position vis-à-vis the notion of leadership. "Real" leaders, if necessary, can do their influencing and transforming mostly without authority, but managers, like it or not, are stuck (or blessed) with authority. Managers these days must do much more cross-connecting, so learning to lead—or at least learning the part about persuading without authority—is very much in order.

Many organizations seem intent on turning their managers into leaders. Their flattened, more networked structures need more semi-autonomous, initiative-taking, connective leaders. So those organizations are trying to make leaders out of managers, a change that should look good to middle managers. After all, who doesn't want to be a leader? On the other side, though, do organizations want to abandon managers in favor of leaders? They'd better not!

Chapter 8 tries to pin down what it takes to be both a manager and a leader in a modern hierarchical organization. It lays out a model of the managing/leading process. The model parses the process into three interconnected phases. Breaking it apart in this way may give us a better handle on the total process. It may help us figure out whether we have what it takes to cope with each of these three phases and the contradictions among them. More important it can perhaps help a manager decide whether he or she really wants to devote a large part of life to managing and leading in a big, top-down hierarchy.

EIGHT

Three Lessons for Manager/Leaders

It's seems clear that modern managers must have some leadership qualities if they are to succeed and help their employees to succeed. So this chapter will adopt the compound word *manager/leader*. If you're already a manager/leader in a large hierarchy—or if you're aiming to become one—the rest of this is for you.

The pages that follow lay out a three-part model of the modern managing/leading process. The model is the best one I know for serving two purposes at the same time: giving you an overview of the modern managing/leading process and doing it in a way that lets you reflect on how your particular interests, beliefs, and abilities fit (or don't fit) with that lifestyle.[1] It will, I hope, cause you to think a bit about how you and your hierarchy are likely to get along over the long pull and about whether you have the inclinations and skills you are likely to need if you plan to make managing/leading your way of life.

The model is quite simple. It can be diagrammed as shown in Figure 8-1.

The broken vertical lines separating the three phases in Figure 8-1 show that the three aren't entirely separable. The boundaries

FIGURE 8-1

The Managing/Leading Process

Phase 1 Pathfinding	Phase 2 Problem Solving	Phase 3 Implementing

dividing them are permeable in both directions. Nor does the 1-2-3 order mean that they need be sequential, although they often are.

Let's begin at phase 3, the implementing phase of the managing/ leading process, and then work backward to the problem-solving and pathfinding phases.

PHASE 3: IMPLEMENTING

Implementing is the action part of managing/leading. Managers are people who do things, make things happen. It's in the third position because usually, but not always, M/Ls act *after* decisions have been made.

Managers' behavior has always been characterized by action. For more than half a century, in fact, different researchers, in different places, with different theoretical perspectives have simply followed managers (that's what the researchers called them, so I'll stick with that label for a short while) to see what they actually do. These observational studies have repeatedly come up with the same action-oriented findings.[2]

For example, managers, then and now, here and there, don't usually work on only one or two things each day; instead, they work on fifteen or twenty different things. They work mostly in short spurts. They hold many brief, informal meetings, at the water cooler or in the corridor. And they work mostly on other people's problems not tasks that they themselves have initiated—problems that customers, suppliers, or people up or down the hierarchy bring to them. Much managerial action, that is to say, is reaction to multiple incoming requests, demands, and crises.

These commonalities, which recur through time and across space, suggest that there really is a common, enduring managerial culture, a culture heavy on phase 3, implementing. Managers don't sit and think all day long. They *do* things, albeit indirectly. Managerial culture is not as strong, perhaps, as the cultures of journalists or professional football players, but it's reasonably clear nonetheless. Such cultures are like selective magnets. They attract certain kinds of people to begin with, and, once they're inside, the culture socializes them still further into these action-focused norms and values.

Here's the first point at which the "leader" part of manager/leaders begins to show up. Manager/leaders act, but they almost always act *indirectly*, with and through other people. Managerial action is almost all social action. M/Ls are social influencers. They don't do things themselves; they get others to do things with and for them. That may seem a callous way to describe the implementing part of the managing/leading process, but it's true. Manager/leaders, in one way or another, must influence other people to do what managers want them to do. That's why organizations have always given their managers authority, and because authority isn't what it used to be, it's also part of the reason that organizations now want to turn managers into leaders.

Implementing, it's worth noting, isn't all sweetness and light. It covers a broad range of actions. Leaders a la Burns and Gardner are likely to be good implementers, but there's only a fine line separating moral forms of implementing from rather sleazy manipulation. Con men (and women) are also likely to be very good social influencers. So are many silken-voiced politicians.

Neophyte M/Ls soon learn that they can neither do their jobs all by themselves nor, despite their authority, simply command people to do them. Their people will do 90 percent of what M/Ls ask of them, if they're asked in an atmosphere of mutual respect. But to implement that last 10 percent—to get those difficult bits done through people—manager/leaders need humanizing, social influencing skills, and that means they have to deal with human *emotionality*.

The Concept of Emotionality

Social influencing is all about people's feelings and emotions. It's about getting people to want to do things, to become motivated, to feel challenged, inspired, or perhaps to feel panicked or frightened.

Social psychologists know a good deal about social influence.[3] One of the things they know is that social influence has much more to do with emotionality than with rationality, more to do with the belly and the heart than with the brain. In such matters, emotion dominates reason. Occasionally, some of us can be persuaded by rational argument, but far less often than one might guess. As every sensible politician knows, we the people are more likely to be influenced by fear, love, greed, and our never-ending search for security than we are by mere facts. In human relationships, anger, jealousy, ambition, and empathy are major triggers of behavioral change.

Hierarchies, however, are, by nature, emotionally backward. The idea of feelings is beyond their ken. That's one of the things that makes it hard for middle-level M/Ls. M/Ls must be savvy about emotionality and the irrationality that often accompanies it. But hierarchies are structurally designed as though people were cool, rational machines, built to do what their "superiors" tell them to do. Hierarchies aren't set up to respond to the quirky emotionality of the human world.

That may be hierarchies' weakest link. Hierarchies' basic inability to incorporate emotionality causes all kinds of trouble at the action end of the managing/leading process. Indeed that's the crack in the dike through which the whole idea of participative management was able to make its initially unwelcomed way into large hierarchies.

So when it comes to the implementing phase of your job, your authority and your school smarts are not nearly enough. What you will also need is a good supply of emotional smarts, an ability to sense and empathize, and to feel generally comfortable in the non-rational world of human emotionality. You might also note that such emotional savvy used to be sloughed off by macho males as "feminine" and therefore inappropriate for the managing job. No more. Now young M/Ls of both sexes had better be tuning up their "feminine" sides—their sensitivity, empathy, and compassion.

What does all this mean in terms of your day-to-day behavior? It means, for one thing, that all of your own on-the-job behavior always—intentionally or not—serves as a model for your people. That's because we learn as much about how we're expected to behave from watching the actual (not the announced) behavior of our M/Ls, from their body language, tones of voice, tensions, and uncertainties. It also means that you'd better do a lot of listening, supporting, and encouraging, even though much of it may, rationally speaking, appear to be a waste of time.

Many M/Ls don't like the whole social-emotional aspect of their jobs. It makes them uncomfortable. They don't like having to sell their ideas, and they don't like to "waste time" having to listen to people's troubles or having to wait until people finally come around to agreeing with what they should have agreed with two hours ago. And some M/Ls may feel so inept at these social skills that they prefer to denigrate them as soft-headed nonsense. HP may have emphasized MBWA (managing by walking around), but many M/Ls prefer Nike's slogan: "Just do it." Only later do they discover that a little walking around can go a long way toward helping them just do it.

Can Social Influencing Be Learned?

How and where can you learn to become a social influencer? Not in the classrooms of most business schools, although you can probably learn a good deal by watching *how* your professors teach as well as *what* they teach. You might also spend time with your university's basketball coach. Or try watching litigating lawyers in action, the ones who must decide whether to select women or men, old folks or young, for a jury, the ones who must think about the subtleties and nuances of the questions they ask and the idiosyncrasies of the witnesses they cross-examine.

Another possibility: Do a stint as a second lieutenant in the infantry. See if you can persuade fifty soldiers to charge enthusiastically up an enemy-held hill. Perhaps you should go on the road for a few days with a traveling salesperson. Or try doing a little selling yourself. There is a classic sales mantra: "You have to sell yourself before you sell your product." Translation: Build a positive emotional relationship with your customer before extolling the rational virtues of your product.

These are ways of learning from experience, more than from books. But now that much is known about the social influencing process, books can also help, and so can seminars and workshops.[4]

PHASE 2: PROBLEM SOLVING

The problem-solving phase of the managing/leading process calls on the M/L's intellectual rather than emotional skills. It's about logical thinking and systematic planning. It is thus mostly systemizing territory. M/Ls must do more than influence other people to do things. They also must make difficult decisions, calculate probabilities, and work out optimal solutions to complicated problems—albeit mostly other people's problems. Manager/leaders must be action-oriented, but they'd also better be able to think rationally and analytically.

The problem-solving phase of the M/L process shares at least one thing in common with the implementing phase. Both try to influence people to do things, but in different ways. Problem solvers do it the hierarchy's way, in two sequential steps: first, by collecting the evidence and making the decision, and then by implementing the decision via hierarchical authority and formal controls. They follow a usually—though not always— sensible rule: Aim first, then fire!

Problem solving is what Robert McNamara (of Ford and the DOD) was great at, and Harold Geneen of ITT, and other much admired and highly analytic business leaders of the 1960s and 1970s. Now, in our new era of nanotechnology, sensible problem solving has become an even more important aspect of the total managing/leading process.

Don't, however, take on the challenge of solving complicated business problems all by yourself. M/Ls who make solo managerial decisions will almost certainly get into trouble when they try to implement those decisions. For that's when you will need the commitment and support of other people. And other people will not necessarily think your baby is as beautiful as you do.

Yet many new M/Ls try to do just that, to make decisions alone. They want to show how smart and decisive they are, so they analyze problems and make quick decisions without consulting the people around them. M/Ls certainly need to develop good phase 2 problem-solving skills, and that's doable. But having learned such skills, they'd better not think that their brilliant decisions will simply implement themselves. Even more important, they'd better not think that their authority will ensure the effective implementation of their decisions. In today's organizations, it won't.

Learning Problem-Solving Skills

Unlike implementing, manager/leader, problem solving is something you will find many opportunities to learn at school and from books. Your math and science courses will certainly help. Problem solving is what much, perhaps most, of an M.B.A. education is about, especially the courses in finance, statistics, microeconomics, and accounting.

These courses teach you how to analyze problems and figure out the best answers, but most of them don't teach you much about how to implement those answers. In fact many of them implicitly assume that analytically good decisions, because they are rationally correct, will somehow implement themselves. They leave much of the complexity of real-world implementing to phase 3 implementing courses—courses in organizational behavior and human resource management—which, unfortunately, often don't teach much about implementing either.

THE DANGEROUS TERRAIN BETWEEN
PROBLEM SOLVING AND IMPLEMENTING

Tread carefully as you travel back and forth between phases 2 and 3: problem solving and implementing. Land mines are buried everywhere in the rocky terrain between these two, especially in the organizations of our new knowledge world. Rookie M/Ls, like Mike of chapter 6, frequently suffer serious wounds trying to negotiate their way through that territory.

You will surely be pressed by the people upstairs—the planners and policy wonks and bean counters—to do more phase 2 problem solving, to crunch the numbers, to run a tighter ship, to get things done by absolute deadlines and within unforgiving budgets. And why not? Those up the hierarchy have handed you a shotgun of authority, haven't they? That's supposed to make it possible for you to implement your phase 2 decisions. Once you know what needs to be done, just aim your weapon and fire. Just do it!

Don't go that route. That shotgun, you'll find, won't get you very far these days. The people in modern hierarchies are imbued with all sorts of weird notions about their own autonomy. They may well demand further explanation. They may argue, or they may simply ignore or circumvent actions on decisions they consider inappropriate. Moreover, their unique abilities and knowledge are critical to getting your work done. So don't cross them. Speak softly and relegate most of your authority to a dusty corner of the attic. Your people know you still have it. They will do most of the routines that they expect they should do. But unless you're forced to, don't even aim your piece, let alone fire off a new plan or policy or other significant change before you've talked things over with the relevant people.

M/Ls who over-concentrate on phase 2 problem solving can be much like Mr. Spock on *Star Trek*. They can be admirably logical but naively un-*psycho*logical. Real people don't always do what logical systemizers can clearly demonstrate to be the correct things to do, a fact that, again and again, seems to shock extreme phase 2 mavens. Thus shocked, the real-life Mr. Spocks often try to recover by laying on even more of what they understand best, systemizing. So to get those stubborn, irrational people to do what the M/L knows they should do, extreme systemizers are likely to tighten controls further. They thereby further rigidify the hierarchy and further alienate those people. Indeed, this circular process has, over the years, helped to steepen and support human hierarchies everywhere.

Humanizing implementers can become emotional when they encounter systemizers who are going in this wrong direction. "You're ignoring a fundamental psychological truth," they complain, "the truth that 'people support what they help to create.' They may very well not support even logically correct solutions that they didn't help to create. Participation is what's needed, not tighter controls. Authority won't do it, except perhaps in emergencies, and in most of those, people will willingly do what's asked of them without weapons pointed at their heads. Get your people involved in planning and decision-making. Come out of your office and away from your work-station. Get out there and mix it up with the real folks. That's the way to add a bit of inspiring leadership to mundane management!"

You had better pay careful attention to such humanizing preaching, but with the clear understanding that you'll have to humanize within a predominantly systemizing, authoritarian hierarchy. So you'll also have to pay attention to problem solvers' favorite words, such as *rationality, rigor,* and *discipline.* You'll have to juggle phases 2 and 3. You'll have to become a problem-solving implementer.

You will probably have to do even more than that. The most important piece of the whole managing/leading puzzle is yet to come. In a large hierarchy, solving the problem and getting its solution implemented are not easy. But what's much harder and far more important is finding the right problem to solve. That's where phase 1, pathfinding, enters the picture.

PHASE 1: PATHFINDING

We come now to the real heart of the managing/leading matter, the phase long ignored by scholars and executives alike. There's more to managing/leading than solving tough problems and implementing their solutions. There's the prior question of choosing the right problems to solve.

Pathfinding is about the front end of the whole M/L process. It's about fuzzy but critical ideas such as *vision, values, imagination,* and *determination.* Pathfinding is therefore very much about *you,* about who you are, what you value, and what you believe is worth doing. It adds to the already complex managerial role by introducing you, the person, into the equation. X, Y, and Z may be what the book or the boss says managers should do, but pathfinding adds who the particular M/L is and what he or she believes, values, and wants. Pathfinding is about leadership, but not about the phase 3 persuading and influencing aspects of leadership. It's about the directions in which leaders choose to lead.

To do pathfinding, you must look into yourself, not just out at the world. Pathfinding is about deciding what you would do if your menu of choices were unlimited or, better yet, if you had no menu at all—only your sense of what you believe to be right and worth doing. Phase 1 pathfinding is about designing the future, not forecasting it, about choosing where you want to go. It's about the leadership side of Bennis's list of differences between managers and leaders, about "doing the right thing" and setting one's "eyes on the horizon."

For a familiar example of why the pathfinding phase is critical, take another look at the U.S. Declaration of Independence. That's a pathfinding document par excellence. Notice how little it takes from phase 2. "We hold these truths to be self-evident," it proclaims, an assertion that must have driven contemporary systemizers up the wall. What the devil are *self-evident* truths? No evidence needed? If you don't have any evidence, how can you claim they're true? Would you go before the executive committee and ask for funding for self-evident truths? Aren't people who talk that way just dreamers and mystics? If you want to know whether or not something's true, don't simply assert it. Go get the facts, run the experiments, figure out the likely ROI. Isn't that what most managers are taught?

Of course, such visionary beliefs, values, and ideals can't be shoved aside like that. Suppose the founders of the United States had not believed those truths to be self-evident. Suppose they had not envisioned a society in which life, liberty, and the pursuit of happiness would reign supreme? For more than two hundred years now, that evidence-free, fact-free, pathfinding vision has guided and directed the problem-solving decisions and implementing actions of even the hardest of our hard-heads.

When we think about pathfinders, great individual leaders are likely to come to mind—Christ, Gandhi, Mohammed, Mother Teresa,

Mandela, King, Meir, and Lincoln, or perhaps visionary leaders of organizations like Hewlett and Packard or Jobs. Pathfinding, it seems, is for such rare and singular men and women, not for us mere mortals.

Wrong! Wrong in two respects: First, note something else about the pathfinding founders of the United States. They were *several* founders—plural not singular, a group, not an individual, and a small, very *hot group* at that. Pathfinding is not for individuals alone, although it is most often associated with individuals. Indeed, small groups are far more likely to carry out effective implementing of organizational visions than are solo individuals.

And pathfinding *is* for us mortals. Pathfinding is about knowing where we want to go, about purpose and direction. Pathfinding does more than add meaning to our lives. It is our strongest defense against the soul-eroding effects of corrosive hierarchies. When we know what we believe and where we want to go, hierarchy cannot seduce us. We can work *in* hierarchies and work *with* them, but we cannot be consumed by them.

This doesn't mean that you should get so involved in your pathfinding vision that you ignore problem solving and implementing. You'll need help from the other two phases in order to thread your way through modern organizational minefields. In fact, if you reexamine the list of great names, you'll notice that every one of them was a very good implementer—a persuader and influencer—as well as a visionary pathfinder. That 1-3 combination is powerful, especially when some rational phase 2 competence is added to the mix.

Visionary Pathfinding: For Senior Executives Only?

Some middle managers, as well as some senior executives, may argue that pathfinding is top management's job; middle managers are not there to envision and imagine. They're managers. Their job is to get done what their seniors envision. That argument may have been somewhat defensible in the pre-information, pre-knowledge world, but it doesn't make much sense now. It's like the old "let's hire a hand" posture of half a century ago. These days the jobs of M/Ls are too multifaceted to try to suppress their individuality. Flattened, networked organizations had better be doing the reverse.

Still, you'd be wise to keep in mind that you are embedded deep inside an authoritarian hierarchy. Your personal visions and values, or your group's, aren't likely to reshape the entire hierarchical giant's direction or purpose, at least not on day one. But neither should you park your soul outside the gate when you go to work in a hierarchy. If you choose your organization wisely, your hierarchy's vision may be quite simpatico with your own. You may then easily find room to fit your beliefs and values within its broad framework. Even if your hierarchy doesn't have a clear vision, you may still find enough space to move in the direction you believe to be right, to manage and lead in accordance with your vision and values.

But if your organization's vision is one you can't abide, or if your organization proclaims Y but behaves X, then you have a problem on your hands. And you had best acknowledge that problem early. Don't delay too long, for if you do, day-to-day hierarchical pressures will begin to blur your vision. These pressures can begin to make wrong look right and turn dreams into nightmares.

PATHFINDERS WHO KNOW HOW TO IMPLEMENT

People who are competent and comfortable with both phases 1 and 3 have a lot going for them. If someone has a clear sense of purpose coupled with an ability to articulate it so persuasively that others voluntarily join up, most of us would probably be willing to label that person a leader. Isn't that the combination that Martin Luther King, Jr., gave to the United States, Mohandas Gandhi gave to India, and Jesus Christ—and the founders of other great religions—bequeathed to large segments of humanity? Isn't that combination also close to a Burns/Gardner/Bennis common denominator of "real" leadership?

Of course it's not only such great public figures who can move from phase 1 to phase 3. Many others can and do. Consider entrepreneurs. Most are passionately committed to their visions. And the successful ones must be effective implementers, persuading venture capitalists to finance them and relevant others enthusiastically to share in implementing their goals.

Note, too, that people who can do *only* phase 1 do not make the history books. Dreamers who cannot bring their dreams at least part way to fruition are only dreamers, not transforming leaders.

Committed humanizers are likely to have mixed feelings about pathfinding. In the abstract, they approve of words such as *vision* and *values,* but many are ambivalent, and properly so, about impassioned individual visionaries who want other people to go where they lead. Some pathfinders—many entrepreneurs among them— aren't very sensitive to these humanistic implementing issues. They're so enamored of their own purposes that it's pretty much their way or the highway.

Humanizers don't particularly like the pathfinding notion's focus mostly on individuals. Humanizers' efforts, after all, encourage collaboration and participation. They prefer using small groups, achieving mutual understanding, and building a sense of common purpose among all of an organization's members. Although they take to the notion of leadership, they aren't smitten by its corollary, followership. They fear that others of us may too quickly abandon our individuality to march as loyal but mindless followers behind a charismatic pathfinder. After all, Adolf Hitler was superb at both phases 1 and 3. So are many not very lovable dictators, cult leaders, and a few CEOs.

There is nothing, however, in any organizational bible that says pathfinding must be the exclusive property of individuals. The founders of the United States were not the only pathfinding group. So were Apple's founding team—Jobs and Wozniak—and Ben Cohen and Jerry Greenfield of Ben & Jerry's. "The history of the world," the sociologist W. E. B. Dubois once wrote, "is the history, not of individuals, but of groups."[5]

PATHFINDERS VERSUS PROBLEM SOLVERS

Think about yourself. If you tend to favor logical, systematic, phase 2 ways of thinking, you may have trouble with the whole pathfinding notion, and vice versa. True-blue problem solvers tend to poohpooh visionary ideas that have no factual, logical basis. Pathfinding is where cultists and screwballs live, people who float too far above solid ground. And pathfinding types see problem solvers as overly conservative, anal-retentive bean counters who are forever tossing obstacles into the path of creativity and imagination.

The stresses and strains between the pathfinding and problem-solving parts of the M/L process are especially apparent in the world of education. Here's one old story that illustrates how the problem-solving way of thinking can bump heads with the pathfinding way. It's a conundrum of the genre you will surely encounter in more serious form at some points in your managerial career.

The tale is about Robert Benchley—editor, author, humorist, essayist—when he was a freshman at Harvard in the early 1900s, and it is composed of two scenes.

> *Scene 1:* Benchley is taking a final exam in Economics 101. He is seated, along with a great mass of other students, at a long table in Harvard's imposing, cathedral-like Memorial Auditorium. Proctors pace, like prison guards, back and forth on high balconies at either end of the great hall. Benchley, like the other students, is hard at work on his answer to this difficult exam question: "Write a five-hundred-word essay on the current economics of the fisheries of Alaska."

> *Scene 2:* It is 3:00 the next morning, in the lamplit study of Economics Professor Mordecai Jones. Professor Jones, all alone, is still wearily grading examination papers. He has just gotten to Benchley's response to the question about Alaskan fisheries. Benchley's essay begins as follows: "I don't know much about the economics of the fisheries of Alaska, but I will give you the fishes' point of view."

The rest of Benchley's answer is a brilliant descriptive piece about what the fish must think and feel about those humans up there worrying about fisheries' economics.

Now to the point of the tale: You are Professor Jones. Your task: Grade Benchley's paper.

There is a serious issue at the heart of this story—a knife-edge pathfinding versus problem-solving issue. If you are a problem-solving phase 2 Professor Jones, you may well decide to give Benchley a failing grade. This was not, after all, a course in creative writing. It was a course in economics. Benchley's paper is utterly inadequate. He simply didn't answer the question. Grade: Zero.

But if, Professor Jones, you have any phase 1 pathfinding in your soul, you will realize what such a failing grade will do. It will punish this creative young man for his divergent, original way of thinking. You'll be telling him that his kind of imaginative intelligence is not valued here. You certainly don't want to do that. Benchley's answer may not be good economics, you reason, but it's a brilliant piece. This kid is hot. His creativity should be encouraged. Grade: 100.

Of course, that direction offers no free lunch either. Benchley, rejoicing in his excellent grade, immediately hurries to tell his classmates all about how he got it. How many witty, unresponsive answers will students turn in the next time Professor Jones gives an exam?

Both formal education and formal hierarchies conspire to drive apart pathfinding and problem solving. Problem solving usually tends toward convergence, toward single best answers. Pathfinding tends to go the other way, toward multiple options and possibilities. But you, M/L, must glue the two back together, for your own sake and for your people's. Otherwise you may have to do what many managers have done in the past: abandon the pathfinding part of yourself and perhaps your people's pathfinding opportunities as well. You may then have to treat the whole M/L process—as educators and executives often still treat it—as simply a phase 2 and phase 3 issue, only problem solving and implementing. That would mean treating the world as a place where the problems-to-be-solved are givens, visible, already there. If you abandon the pathfinding phase you will also abandon the problem *making*, problem *creating* part of the process. That's no way to move forward or to find meaning in your work. Without phase 1, what will then be left of *you*?

PUTTING THE THREE PHASES TOGETHER

Not every manager/leader will become a super combination of path-finding Dr. King, problem-solving Mr. McNamara, and implementing President Lyndon Johnson (for he, in his unique way, was a superb implementer). Such a combination would be great, but few of us can realistically aspire to top grades in all three phases. As a modern manager, however, you had better, at a minimum, comprehend and appreciate the relevance and importance of all three phases. Each of us can surely try for reasonable grades in one or more of the three and can also welcome—indeed seek out—others who can help us handle the phases we ourselves may not do very well.

Such appreciation of diverse ways of viewing the world is perhaps especially difficult when we're just starting out, or at least it seems that way to me. If I were a student at MIT today, I would try much harder *not* to scorn "the other"—those systemizers down on the first floor—as my colleagues and I did then. When we were beginning to form our third-floor participative beliefs, denigrating the first floor's analytic ways of thinking helped us to reassure ourselves that we were "the chosen." We knew Truth. Unfortunately, our zeal also kept us from comprehending what truth the first-floor people were searching for.

Nor would I any longer devalue and disparage as crazies those with phase 1 faiths unsupported by my kind of Western empiricism—not, at least, until I had first tried very hard to understand their ways.

So integrating all three phases of the managing/leading process isn't easy, especially when you're hemmed in by the hierarchy's constricting regulations. These three chunks just don't fit neatly with one another. It takes a lot of negotiating, compromising, and creative intermixing to make them work together. Implementing and problem solving require quite different ways of looking at the same things, and so do problem solving and pathfinding. And even though pathfinding and implementing share much common ground, they have some deep differences, too.

In most organizations, and in business schools as well, the pathfinding part of the M/L process is still neglected. Indeed, much of management education has omitted phase 1 entirely. Until recently, analytic problem solving dominated B-school curricula, a reality that actively discouraged pathfinding. We have generally sent our students in search of "correct" phase 2 answers rather than interesting or imaginative phase 1 questions.

In keeping with that educational tradition, therefore, but with quite different intent, this chapter concludes with a short quiz:

Now, rookie (or veteran) manager/leader, rate yourself on each of the three phases of the managing/leading process. Don't worry about whether you're tagged as a leader or as a manager. Use the three-phase model to think about what you may need if you are to work effectively and to gain some sense of personal worth as you do your thing amidst the pains, pressures, and pleasures of a big, modern hierarchy.

Try answering the following questions using the usual scale of 1 (low) to 9 (high):

1. Phase 3, implementing: Rate your effectiveness in getting things done with and through people. Are you persuasive? Can you read people? Are you a good negotiator? Do you like to mix and network? Do the people you supervise willingly do what you want them to do? Do you operate comfortably in small face-to-face groups? Do you like bringing people together? Can you influence up as well as down?

   Low 1 - 2 - 3 - 4 - 5 - 6 - 7 - 8 - 9 High

2. Phase 2, problem solving: Rate your ability to think in an orderly, systematic, logical way. Do you get the facts before you make decisions? Do you keep careful records? Are you a systematic planner? Are you OK with math? Do others see you as sharp-minded and clear-headed? Are you rational, logical? Do you sweat the details?

   Low 1 - 2 - 3 - 4 - 5 - 6 - 7 - 8 - 9 High

3. Phase 1, pathfinding: Rate your vision, values, and sense of purpose. Are you imaginative, creative? Are you pretty sure

about what you want to do with your life? Do you have a deep sense of integrity? Do you hold strong beliefs and values? Do others see you as an independent thinker, someone who marches to his or her own drummer?

Low 1 - 2 - 3 - 4 - 5 - 6 - 7 - 8 - 9 High

Now, three more questions: First, did you rate yourself reasonably high on all three phases? Second, even if you didn't score high on *any* of them, do you believe that all three are important for effective managing/leading in large hierarchical organizations? If you think not, then why not? Third, can you find ways to improve your skills on the phases on which you rated yourself low?

If your answer to either of the first two questions is affirmative, then the model says that you have a shot at becoming an effective manager/leader appropriate to the organizational world in which we now live. That's because a yes to the first question suggests that you have it all and that you may be able to weave your way through a complex hierarchy without losing your soul. Yes to the second question suggests two positives: First, you will not surround yourself with clones but instead will have the good sense to seek out and value people who have what you don't. And second, you will go to question 3 and think about how you can learn to do better at the phases you don't do very well.

Chapter 9, the final chapter of this book, is a reprise, but it also raises some questions about issues closely related to pathfinding in authoritarian hierarchies, questions about modern managers' moral duties and responsibilities.

NINE

Hierarchies, Managers, and Morality

For managers, hierarchies generate imbalanced power relationships. Managers are simultaneously dependent on their more powerful superiors and more powerful than their dependent subordinates. That dual role can demoralize managers in two senses: It can *demoralize*—dishearten and demotivate them—because they are less powerful, and it may *demoralize*—corrupt and debase them—because they are also more powerful. Because they occupy both sides of these power relationships, managers must deal with both dangers.

So these final pages try to look beyond the bottom line, to the psychological and moral issues that hierarchies always entail, to matters of managerial self-esteem, integrity, morality, and social responsibility. They urge managers to stay real, to be alert to and savvy about their hierarchical surroundings and the authoritarian settings in which they work. And they remind managers that their roles involve duties beyond the immediate job at hand—duties to colleagues, to employees, to society at large, and to themselves.

FIRST, SOME CONCLUSIONS

Let's begin by revisiting our main theme and a tentative conclusion: For many decades, humanizing scholars have been forecasting the demise of large organizational hierarchies, asserting that the few still breathing are—blessedly—the last of their line. Some of these observers have done more than forecast. They have simply pronounced hierarchies dead and have published their obituaries.

In fact, however, large, top-down, human hierarchies are not even in ill health. Recent advances in technology may well have done more to invigorate than to decimate them. Hierarchies are still with us and they are still basically authoritarian systems.

The hard-fisted authoritarianism of the past has been pretty much supplanted by far gentler varieties, some of them so gentle that newcomers may think authoritarianism isn't even there. But it *is* there. For while humanizing forces have been upgrading hierarchies' humanism, systemizing forces have been busily inventing new methods of enforcing organizational discipline and good order, thereby reinforcing top-down hierarchical structures.

Middle managers can easily find themselves caught in the crossfire between these two broad, warring forces, humanizing and systemizing. The two constitute a kind of yang and yin of organizational life, intertwined and inseparable and yet opposites. Humanizers envision egalitarian organizations, innovative, crisis-competent, sparkling with creativity and high interpersonal trust. They have developed a large set of managerial theories and methods that this book has collectively called *participative management*. And by teaching these ideas, humanizers have affected significant humanizing changes in the behavior of managers at all levels.

Systemizers, too, have exerted great influence, perhaps even more at senior than at middle levels. Systemizers' eyes are trained on the whole organization more than on its human molecules. For them, people are one of several replaceable parts for the smoothly functioning organizations that they keep trying to build. To the degree that humans remain economical resources, systemizers will put up with their continued, albeit rather disruptive, presence. With technology's help, modern systemizing has sharply improved middle and top managers' ability to communicate, measure, control, and forecast. I have called that broad package *analytic management.*

Large organizations have gone off in both humanizing and systemizing directions: They have loosened and teamed while they simultaneously continue to tighten and control. This ill-matched combination makes up a large part of the work-related, psychological, and moral tangle that modern middle manager/leaders must confront.

Recently, a third force, the task-impassioned small *hot group,* has entered the fray. Its wide-open, innovative style adds complexity to the scene. Hot group members don't fuss about humanizing relationships or systemizing cost controls. Their total beings are pointed fixedly at their task. And although hot groups don't work as hierarchies, many work within them or eventually themselves grow into them. The husbandry and effective use of such groups—from task forces to self-managed teams to communities of interest—have now also been added to the mixture on the middle manager's plate.

With all three of these managerial approaches speeding in different directions and all three operating under big organizations' somewhat muted authoritarian umbrellas, modern middle managers have their hands, and their heads, full.

Hierarchies Aren't All Bad

In many ways, top-down business hierarchies are quite good for all concerned, for middle managers, for the societies in which such organizations live, and for the people who work in them. Their social positives offset many of their personal negatives. Hierarchies remain the most workable and effective structures humans have yet invented for performing large, enduring, complicated tasks. It would be difficult indeed to manufacture and distribute large numbers of tractors, televisions, or telescopes without hierarchies, just as it would be difficult for a community of any size to govern itself hierarchy-free.

Although we rail against hierarchies, they provide managers, and many others, with a multitude of things they want. They provide us with an illusory haven of safety and security, or at least some of them still do. Hierarchies set up ladders to success that we achievement-driven types want to climb. A manager's place in a hierarchy defines a large part of his or her personal identity. Although they don't do it often enough, hierarchies can even provide cognitive platforms that permit us to imagine and then accomplish what we could only imagine without them.

It is not surprising that organizational hierarchies serve many human needs. We are the ones who built them. They are products of some of our most valued human qualities: our irrepressible curiosity and our drive to achieve. Many have been assembled from scratch by just the kinds of people the rest of us admire—autonomous, creative, entrepreneurial people. The trouble usually comes at the next stage, when those of us inside the house that Granddad built try to emulate Granddad. Then we often find that expressions of similar autonomy, creativity, and entrepreneurial spirit are not welcome.

SOME CLOSING THOUGHTS FOR THE MODERN MANAGER/LEADER

I have spent much of this book outlining some of the daunting complexities that confront today's manager/leader. Here are a few additional thoughts you may want to mull over as you make your way through your three dimensional hierarchical maze.

Never Forget That You Work in an Authoritarian Hierarchy

No matter how high or low you may sit on the hierarchical ladder and no matter your personal preference, authority will surely be everywhere around you, and on you, too. You cannot rub off or wash away your authority. You may prefer to work in non-authoritarian ways, but you can't get all the way there from here.

Whether you need it or not, whether you want it or not, your managerial authority is the force that will always be with you. It will be, despite protests to the contrary, the most salient fact of your managerial life. Your particular hierarchy may not be like all those other monsters. It may be a kind, humane place to spend your working life. Nevertheless, it is still a hierarchy, and when pressures mount it will, as it must, show its true authoritarian colors. Is that too harsh a statement? Perhaps. If I overstate the case, scale it back a notch or two—but not three or four.

To complicate matters even further, your authoritarian hierarchy is embedded within a larger democratic society, a society that actively espouses antiauthoritarian values. Since early childhood, your family, school, church, and community have imbued you with nonauthoritarian, egalitarian beliefs. They have taught you that all men—and recently, women and minorities, too—are created equal, that it is wrong to bully or coerce others, that you should appreciate diversity, not only in race and gender but also in points of view. Then you grow up and go to work, there to discover that big organizations are anything but exemplars of such values.

For middle managers—and often for top managers—this mismatch looms large. The authoritarian demands of your role don't jibe with the values you have been taught. Many hierarchies are aware, at some semiconscious level, of that disparity, so they powder and perfume themselves to obscure their underlying unattractiveness. They must behave in authoritarian, hierarchical ways if they are to function effectively, but they must mute that authoritarianism to make life in hierarchies look—and in some cases actually be—reasonably consistent with society's standards.

Even today's senior executives, after all, grew up with democratic values. It is in everyone's interest to minimize hierarchies' top-down authoritarianism. Unfortunately, neither hierarchical organizations nor their individual managers can quite get rid of it. Everyone in the organization knows it's there.

This doesn't mean that your personal authority—your bit of the whole authoritarian system—is no more than a crown of thorns. Authority can be extremely and positively useful, but with the paradoxical quality of being most effective when used least. Experienced managers know that. They exercise their authority sparingly, and when they do, the good ones use it in the interest of the whole group and not in the interest of their egos.

Veteran managers also know that their authority invariably distorts their relations with people down and up the hierarchical ladder. These can never be relationships between equals. They are always, to some degree, power relationships, and this means that—as with parent-child relationships—valid communication will be difficult. Wise managers calibrate their authority's role in these relationships and compensate for the distortions it creates. They develop authoritative presence—the ability to sense and deal comfortably with their authoritarian surroundings, to correct for hierarchies' asymmetries, and to make their way through hierarchies' minefields.

Be aware of your authority, but also beware of it. Don't count on using very much of it to get work done, not in today's hierarchies. Managing now requires horizontal as well as vertical influence and action. It requires connectivity, persuasion, and collaboration, inside and outside the organization. Exercising direct authority—pulling rank—in such mutually dependent settings can be more than useless. It can be counterproductive.

So You Want to Be a Leader . . .

Few managers want to be viewed as authoritarian martinets. They, and you, would surely rather be seen as leaders, as people who exude an aura of vision, competence, and integrity. "Real" leaders don't lead with big sticks of authority. That's dictatorship, not leadership. Leaders, we are told, have a sense of what needs to be done and can persuade and convince others to help them do it.

This leadership idea can cause a conundrum for you middle managers. You aren't just plain folks. You are managers in authoritarian hierarchies. You have work to get done and deadlines to meet. And you are aglow with the neon marker of your authority. So if much of leading means influencing *without* authority, and if managers like you can't shed their authority, you start with a leadership handicap. For managers, that is, leadership has some of the qualities of another relationship: love. Does she (or he) love me for myself or only for my body? Does my group follow me for my leadership skills, or are they just bowing to my authority? Separating the one from the other isn't always easy.

There may be a way out of this dilemma. Perhaps you shouldn't trouble yourself about whether or not you're a "real" leader. You may be better off accepting your authority's costs and taking advantage of its benefits. You can also try hard to develop all the non-authoritarian leadership skills you can muster, calling upon your authority only on the rare occasions when you feel you must. By first acknowledging the fact of your managerial authority and using it with grace and understanding, you may still find satisfaction and meaning while working in an authoritarian hierarchy.

Such a blend of managing and leading would also serve your whole organization well. Organizations are forever sounding off about how their managers should be leaders, but they never seem to worry about leaders becoming managers. Compared with shining, heroic leaders, just plain managers often look dull and uninteresting. Yet heaven help the organization whose every manager has abandoned the solid ground of managership to chase the beckoning star of leadership. Who would be left to meet the payroll?

So don't fret about whether or not you're a "real" leader. Think instead about what you will need if you are to become an effective combination of the two, a manager/leader.

Doing the Whole Managing/Leading Job

If you want to become a combination manager and leader, just what do you have to learn? A chapter ago, this book suggested a three-phase answer to that question. To combine the two, it proposed, managers should try to become effective *implementers,* skillful at getting things done through people. They should also try to become effective *problem solvers:* logical thinkers, planners, and strategists. And third, managers who would become leaders would also be well advised to do some serious *pathfinding:* looking into themselves, imagining and envisioning, choosing the right problems before trying to make decisions or to implement actions.

That front-end pathfinding phase has been much neglected by businesses as well as business schools. Pathfinding is about the future we want to create rather than the one we try to discover. One of my very wise colleagues used to say, "The future is *not.*" He meant that the future isn't history in reverse. It's not just lying out there, waiting for us to find it. We must design it, create it, build it. That's pathfinding, the imaginative, purposive, even spiritual root of the managing/leading process.

If you can learn to be pretty good at all three phases, this book has suggested, you'll probably have much of what's needed to do today's managing/leading job. That's a tall order, because you'll have to go to quite different places to learn each one. Of course, most of us never get to be good at all three. So that leaves you with three choices: You can learn to get better at the phases in which you're weak, or you can connect with and appreciate others who have skills in your weaker phases. Or you can do both, because trying to learn different perspectives may help you to appreciate all of them.

WHAT KIND OF LEADER DO YOU WANT TO BE?

There are leaders, and there are leaders. There are loud leaders and quiet ones, strong, take-charge leaders and gently persuasive ones. There are Pattons and Churchills and Stalins and Maos. And there are also Mother Teresas and Nelson Mandelas and Václav Havels and Martin Luther Kings. What sort of leader do you want to be?

How About a Connective Leader?

Here's a suggestion. One kind of leader whom organizations and the world will surely need more of is the *connective* kind. John Gardner—himself an effective connective leader (he founded, among other things, Common Cause, an influential, nonpartisan public policy organization)—made a critically important point about managerial authority. "Within a more or less *isolated* organization," he wrote, "authority . . . is a potent weapon, always there, even if the leader chooses to use it with a light hand. . . . But in a tumultuous, swiftly changing environment . . . the hierarchical position of leaders within their own system is of limited value, because some of the most critically important tasks require lateral leadership—boundary-crossing leadership—involving groups over whom they have no control. . . . They must do what they can to lead without authority."[1]

In modern hierarchical organizations, managers no longer manage only their own shows. Instead, they must tie into all kinds of horizontal and diagonal networks. Jean Lipman-Blumen points this out and goes a step further. "A new wind is blowing," she writes, "a wind that is changing the leadership climate around the world. . . . It is a time marked by two contradictory forces, *interdependence* and *diversity* pulling in opposite directions."[2]

These issues—interdependence and diversity—come close to the heart of the matter. If you want to figure out whether or not your boss is something of a leader as well as a manager, check out how effective she or he is in working *outside* your unit as well as inside. And check yourself out the same way. How well do you make out with peers, customers, and other groups—diverse people over whom you have no authority but on whom you are to some degree dependent? If you can successfully find common ground with people outside your group jointly to do what you believe is right, you may be on track for the advanced title of connective manager/leader.

Connective leadership is something humanizers like. Some systemizers like it, too, because systemizers can see their kind of value—rational, economic value—in collaborating with others toward common goals. Connective leaders seek out common ground, areas where collaborative relationships can pay off for all concerned. They can be competitive when necessary, but they don't set out to beat others. They set out to build, to succeed with the full understanding that their success need not require others' failure. They cut across traditional boundaries, form alliances, and spot connections where others see only differences.

President George Herbert Walker Bush behaved connectively when he formed a broad international coalition in the first Iraq War. He telephoned, visited, and chatted up the leaders of other countries' hierarchies—their prime ministers, presidents, and kings. His senior staff did likewise, sounding out potential allies and establishing close relationships before they took on Saddam.

The Bush #1's coalition was a temporary one. It disintegrated following the crisis. Some critics complained about that. They wanted a permanent coalition. But the formation of temporary coalitions is characteristic of connective leaders and quite appropriate to the new world. Connective leaders form task groups, often hot ones, assembled to perform a specific task. They pull together people who share a common interest in one task even though the group members may not share interest in another. When the job at hand is concluded, the group often disperses. Then other coalitions may be put together for other tasks.

Why? It's because the world we live in is impermanent and interconnected. Even "isolated" small hot groups can't do much if they're truly isolated. They need connections, and modern technology makes it easy to form connections with relevant people anywhere in the world. They may even need connections to traditional competitors, for in today's environment competing hierarchies cannot be treated, simplistically, as enemies and nothing else.

Connectives reach out to other leaders—leaders in other organizations and other leaders within their own organization. They build networks. They use social instrumental achieving styles. They are political in the sense that they use themselves and their social and other relationships to get things done. We Americans and Northern Europeans take pride in our meritocracies, where ability is the key to success. We have tended to look down our noses, at least nominally, at people who use their "connections" to get themselves or their relatives into schools or jobs or country clubs. You may want to examine that broad prejudice more closely. You may want to parse it into its positives and negatives and select the positives. That's particularly true in the world of work. Leaders don't always have to charge ahead on great stallions. They can persuade more quietly, via networks and personal relationships. If they do so in the interest of the group, and not in their own self-interest, it's a sensible way to behave, isn't it?

Connectivity Up, Competition Down

Consider for a moment not only the process of leading but also its purpose. Leaders, we are told again and again, should lead by persuading and serving as models for their people. But we have also wanted something else from our leaders. We have wanted our leaders to *win*. We've wanted them to lead our team to victory. We have tended, that is, to equate successful leadership with competitive success. That may be why many of those we revere as great leaders were leaders in wartime, when we were both anxious and competitive. Would Churchill have been anointed a great leader if the British had lost World War II? And notice how many of the presidents we Americans most esteem held office during wars that our side won: Washington, Lincoln, Teddy Roosevelt, Wilson, FDR.

Winning is about *competing.* Hierarchical organizations have thrived on competition. In our shrinking global village, however, ever-accelerating technology is pushing all of us—all of us—into unprecedented interdependence. In such a world, the old competitive engine doesn't have the horsepower to do the job. Both within organizational hierarchies and among them, connections, common causes, and combinations have increasingly marked recent decades. Managers like you may still need to win competitive battles, but you will need, perhaps even more, to go the other way: to build and use alliances and connections.

Please also notice that although cross-connections, networks, and multidisciplined teams will almost certainly make up more and more of your working world—indeed of the whole organizational world—such connectivity does not obviate the hierarchy. Your organizational hierarchy remains the base camp from which you will continue to do your connecting and competing, with only minimal help from your formal authority and with the hierarchy's controlling eye always keeping close watch.

HIERARCHIES, MANAGING, AND MORALITY

It's only a short trip from managerial pathfinding and connective leading to the issue of managerial morality. Both your pathfinding behavior and your leadership style are expressions of who and what you are. They are presentations to the world of the kind of person you hold yourself to be, of what you believe is right and what is wrong. Although this book has raised a few such moral questions, it has not given them the emphasis they deserve. Let's not let it end that way.

Here, for example, is a moral issue that may arise, unrecognized, early in your managerial career. Understandably (but wrongly), you may at first feel more gung-ho about your work than about the people around and beneath you. You may be eager to demonstrate to the folks up the hierarchy how much you can accomplish and how fast you can accomplish it. With experience, however, you will learn, or should learn, that business isn't really all business. Your managerial responsibilities extend well beyond next quarter's results. Along with your star of authority, you also carry a symbolic shepherd's crook, signaling your responsibility as a caretaker of vital aspects of other people's lives. In the long run, that simple shepherd's crook may well turn out to be more important to your own life and career than multiple stars on your epaulets.

Managerial Duty

Consultants, academics, and executives seem largely to ignore the *duty* aspect of the manager's job. Old textbooks on management used to sound off regularly about it. Authority and responsibility, they taught, were conjoined twins. When I was a graduate student, my classmates and I pooh-poohed such talk as meaningless jargon. Yet the idea that authority must be counterbalanced by responsibility remains relevant for today's managers.

Two messages, not just one, were being sent by that old dictum. The first message: Authority implies accountability. If you wear a star of authority, you are the responsible party, the one who must take the heat if the job isn't done right, and, of course, you should also garner the rewards if it is. That idea is still pretty much with us.

But a second all-but-forgotten and more important message implicitly accompanied that authority/responsibility rule: a moral message. The responsibility that attaches to authority also refers to the authority-holder's duty to the people in his or her group. That message urged managers to treat their authority as a burden of responsibility not as a gift of personal power. The idea that managerial duty accompanies managerial authority seems largely to have been brushed aside by many contemporary organizations and by contemporary management education, too. The graduating M.B.A., regrettably, takes no equivalent to the M.D.'s Hippocratic Oath.

And a small addendum here: Business schools probably deserve at least a piece of the blame for the recent explosion of corporate turpitude. A great splurge of analytic systemizing dominated the B-school scene from the 1960s well into the 1990s.[3] That orgy bred an M.B.A. population hypnotically fixated on the bottom line. That wasn't, in itself, a great failing. The failing lay in the absence of a sufficiently strong counterpoint from the humanizing side. For a couple of decades our "best" business schools were turning out too many students with lopsided perspectives on the real world, people with many numbers in their heads but little compassion in their hearts. Fortunately, that unintended self-serving binge appears to be winding down.

On matters of managerial duty, you and your organization might do well to take a page from the military's book. Military organizations put managers' responsibility for their people front and center, loud and clear. Every new second lieutenant knows that his or her primary responsibility is for the welfare of the people in the unit.

Would it were so in business and industry. There, next quarter's results often take precedence over everything else. Managers are not solely to blame for that. We educators, senior executives, and the "system" are also miscreants. We have too long lionized financial and positional success while neglecting, even denigrating, that old but broad definition of *responsibility*. Managers who have been gifted with authority should carry responsibility, including significant responsibility for the well being of their organization's people, its ethics, and its societal relations. So, manager, whether or not you're asked to, think about shouldering yet another duty: not the non-duty of behaving decently—that's a given—but the duty of helping to promulgate decency throughout your organization.

Managers who do not view their people's welfare and their organization's morality as major responsibilities will sooner or later learn, the hard way, that these are practical as well as moral matters.

Dependency works in both directions. The law of reciprocity applies. If you don't put your people's well-being high on your duty list, they will not put you high on theirs. And if you don't put your organization's morality high on your duty list, the world may stop putting it high on theirs. Then try getting good work done!

Duty to Yourself

Every manager in a large hierarchical organization will surely encounter many moral curveballs in the course of his or her career. Inescapable dilemmas will arise, moments when your personal integrity is on the line, when you must make a binary choice. At such times, you must either do your duty to yourself and to your personal standards or else "modify" your standards to protect status or income. It takes ego strength to maintain your authenticity in such critical situations. Failure to do so entails many costs, not the least of which is an enduring, gnawing sense that your integrity has been irreparably defiled.

Some manager/leaders confront those moral crises less frequently than others. Some regularly emit such strong signals that their high ethical standards become well known and are seldom challenged. A few don't encounter such problems for the opposite reason: Their standards are so low that almost nothing ever challenges them.

Many experienced managers with high standards use their understanding of themselves and their organizations to help them make their way through ethical minefields. They develop the authoritative presence that helps them cope with such dilemmas, maintaining both integrity and position. Others, after encountering one too many such episodes, choose to exit the offending hierarchy. Despite great personal costs, they opt for a different way of life. And some just give in, to become feeble pawns of their hierarchy's will.

That last choice generally ends unhappily for both manager and organization. Over time, it almost always leads to one or both of two outcomes: These managers may end up as organizational deadwood, stripped of most of their power, relegated to their organization's bleak wastelands, there to suffer the pity, contempt, or indifference of their peers. Or, more dangerously, such figures become preoccupied with the only power remaining to them, their formal authority. Beware such men and women! They may warrant compassion, but they're dangerous. They toady up and dictate down.

Big Hierarchical Organizations Are Still Deviant Members of Society

Here, finally, is a variant of a quasi-syllogism from an earlier chapter:

Large human organizations are hierarchies.
Human hierarchies are authoritarian systems.
Many large human organizations live in non-authoritarian societies.
Therefore, those organizations are out of sync with their societies.
True or false?

If the answer is true (and mostly it *is* true), then big authoritarian hierarchies in non-authoritarian societies are outliers, deviant members of their communities. Does that mean we should tar and feather them and drive them out? There's an old Navy dictum that goes "Shape up or ship out!" It is right and proper that societies press their hierarchical organizations to shape up, but do we really want them to ship out? No way! We need those giants. They do great things for us.

Still, we can certainly keep needling them to become better citizens, to bring themselves closer to society's espoused values. We can keep pressing them to get with it, to humanize themselves more, to focus more on connecting, even as they continue to systemize. Some brave organizational leaders have long since demonstrated that it is possible to move that way. It may be harder now than it was even a few years ago, because the speeding world and accelerating technology generally drive hierarchies in the other direction. But it can be done. Indeed, the world makes the counterpoint of positive humanizing ever more imperative.

There are many good reasons for pushing organizations toward something closer to democracy, but here, surely, is the best one of all. Organizations, like their leaders, should travel the humanizing route simply because of one of those self-evident truths: It's just the right thing to do, the decent way to go. Senior executives, perhaps even more than juniors, need to be reminded again and again that their positions entail far more fundamental duties than the mere maximization of stockholder value.[4]

Big hierarchies are here to stay, and for a while, at least, they will continue to be populated by people like you, manager/leaders, and by us, your fellow humans. So whether we are high or low on our hierarchical ladders, let's behave like responsible, civilized human beings. Let's help make our organizations—hierarchical though they may be—more enriching habitats for other responsible, civilized human beings. Top-down, hierarchical organizations may be inevitable, but they needn't be toxic.

NOTES

Preface

1. Harold J. Leavitt, "Some Effects of Certain Patterns of Communication on Group Performance," *Journal of Abnormal and Social Psychology* 46, 1 (1951); Harold J. Leavitt and Bernard M. Bass, "Organizational Psychology," *Annual Review of Psychology* 15 (1964); Jean Lipman-Blumen and Harold J. Leavitt, *Hot Groups: Seeding Them, Feeding Them, and Using Them to Ignite Your Organization* (New York: Oxford University Press, 1999).

Introduction

1. *The Catholic Encyclopedia,* vol. VII (New York: Robert Appleton Co., 1910).

2. Elemér Hankiss, *Fears and Symbols: An Introduction to the Study of Western Civilization* (Budapest: Central European University Press, 2001), 51, 52.

3. Quoted in Warren Bennis, *Why Leaders Can't Lead: The Unconscious Conspiracy Continues* (San Francisco: Jossey-Bass, 1989), 152–153.

4. Gifford Pinchot, "An Alternative to Hierarchy," *Leader to Leader* 10 (1998), 41.

5. Kenneth Cloke and Joan Goldsmith, *The End of Management and the Rise of Organizational Democracy* (San Francisco: Jossey-Bass, 2002), 4. For a very different recent view, acknowledging hierarchy, see Samuel A. Culbert and John B. Ullmen, *Don't Kill the Bosses!: Escaping the Hierarchy Trap* (San Francisco: Berrett-Koehler, 2001).

6. Nitin Nohria, "Mary Parker Follett's View on Power, the Giving of Orders, and Authority: An Alternative to Hierarchy or a Utopian Ideology?" in *Mary Parker Follett—Prophet of Management: A Celebration of Writings from the 1920s,* ed. Pauline Graham (Cambridge, MA: Harvard Business School Press, 1996).

7. Thomas A. Stewart, *Intellectual Capital: The New Wealth of Organizations* (New York: Doubleday, 1997), 182.

8. See, for example, Albert-László Barabási, *Linked: The New Science of Networks* (New York: Perseus, 2002).

9. For a fine analysis of the connection between people and productivity, see Jeffrey Pfeffer, *The Human Equation: Building Profits by Putting People First* (Boston: Harvard Business School Press, 1998).

Chapter 1

1. Erich Fromm, *Escape from Freedom* (New York: Avon, 1941).

2. F. J. Roethlisberger, *The Elusive Phenomena: An Autobiographical Account of My Work in the Field of Organizational Behavior at the Harvard Business School,* ed. George F. F. Lombard (Boston: Harvard Business School, 1977), 165–166.

3. See, for example, Roderick M. Kramer, "The Harder They Fall," *Harvard Business Review* (October 2003), 58–66.

4. Personal communication with anonymous source.

5. Thanks to Diane Coutu of *Harvard Business Review* for the GE story.

6. James C. Collins and Jerry I. Porras, *Built to Last: Successful Habits of Visionary Companies* (New York: Harper Collins, 1994).

Chapter 2

1. Russel L. Ackoff, *The Democratic Corporation: A Radical Prescription for Recreating Corporate America and Rediscovering Success* (New York: Oxford University Press, 1994). See especially Chapter 4, "The Circular Organization."

2. This idea is elaborated in Ernest Becker, *Escape from Evil* (New York: The Free Press, 1975).

3. The Conference Board, *Special Consumer Survey Report: Job Satisfaction on the Decline* (July, 2002).

4. Quoted in Daniel T. Rodgers, *The Work Ethic in Industrial America, 1850–1920* (Chicago: University of Chicago Press, 1979), 35.

5. See a fine little book by Robert W. Fuller, *Somebodies and Nobodies: Overcoming the Abuse of Rank* (Gabriola Island, BC, Canada: New Society Publishers, 2003). It goes after hierarchy from a somewhat different perspective.

6. John De Graaf, "Workweek Woes," *New York Times,* 12 April 2003, A13. His source is the International Labor Organization.

7. Joanne B. Ciulla, *The Working Life: The Promise and Betrayal of Modern Work* (New York: Three Rivers Press, 2000), 223.

8. Alexis de Tocqueville, *Democracy in America* (New York: Alfred A. Knopf, 1945).

9. Jean Lipman-Blumen, *Connective Leadership: Managing in a Changing World* (New York: Oxford University Press, 2000). See especially Chapter 11.

10. A. Bartlett Giamatti, *Take Time for Paradise: Americans and Their Games* (New York: Summit Books, 1990).

11. Rudyard Kipling, "Her Majesty's Servants," in *The Jungle Book* (New York: William Morrow, 1995).

12. Herbert Simon, *The Sciences of the Artificial* (Cambridge, MA: MIT Press, 1969), 188–189.

13. Ibid.

14. *Fortune,* 20 January 2003, 127ff.

Chapter 3

1. Alfred J. Marrow, David G. Bowers, and Stanley Seashore, *Management by Participation: Creating a Climate for Personal and Organizational Development* (New York: Harper and Row, 1967).

2. Editorial, *New York Times,* 30 July 2003.

3. Todd Buchholz, "All Bets Are Off," op-ed piece, *New York Times,* 31 July 2003, A25. Buchholz, it should be made clear, is criticizing the Pentagon proposal.

4. Reuven Brenner, "A Safe Bet," *Wall Street Journal,* 1 August 2003, A8.

5. Temple Burling, *You Can't Hire a Hand and Other Essays* (Ithaca, NY: New York State School of Industrial and Labor Relations, 1950).

6. E. D. Hirsch, Jr., Joseph P. Kett, and James Trefil, *The New Dictionary of Cultural Literacy: What Every American Needs to Know* (Boston: Houghton Mifflin Company, 2002).

7. Upton Sinclair, Frederick Winslow Taylor, letters to the editor, *The American Magazine* 72, May and June, 1911.

8. Ibid.

9. Ibid.

10. Harold J. Leavitt and Thomas L. Whisler, "Management in the 1980s," *Harvard Business Review* (November–December 1998).

11. See, for example, Simon Head, *The New Ruthless Economy: Work and Power in the Digital Age* (New York: Oxford University Press, 2003). He makes a strong case that IT has not released hierarchies' people but instead has tightened restrictions on their behavior.

12. Bill Joy, "Why the Future Doesn't Need Us," *WIRED* 8.04, April 2000, 238–262.

13. Ray Kurzweil, *The Age of Spiritual Machines: When Computers Exceed Human Intelligence* (New York: Viking Penguin, 1999).

14. *New York Times Magazine,* 29 September 1996, 216.

15. *Computer and Internet Dictionary* (Redmond, WA: Microsoft Corporation, 1997).

Chapter 4

1. Pauline Graham, ed., *Mary Parker Follett—Prophet of Management: A Celebration of Writings from the 1920s* (Boston: Harvard Business School Press, 1995); Elton Mayo, *The Human Problems of an Industrial Civilization* (New York: The Macmillan Company, 1933); and F. J. Roethlisberger and William J. Dickson, *Management and the Worker* (Cambridge, MA: Harvard University Press, 1939).

2. Norbert Wiener, *The Human Use of Human Beings: Cybernetics and Society* (Cambridge, MA: Da Capo Press, 1988).

3. Jean Lipman-Blumen, "Role De-differentiation as a System Response to Crisis," *Sociological Inquiry* 43, no. 2 (1973).

4. See, for example, Carl F. Frost, John H. Wakely, and Robert A. Ruh, *The Scanlon Plan for Organization Development: Identity, Participation, and Equity* (East Lansing: Michigan State University Press, 1974).

5. See, for example, William A. Pasmore, *Designing Effective Organizations: The Sociotechnical Systems Approach* (New York: Wiley, 1988).

6. Robert W. Fuller, *Somebodies and Nobodies: Overcoming the Abuse of Rank* (Gabriola Island, B.C., Canada: New Society Publishers, 2003).

7. William G. Ouchi, *Theory Z: How American Companies Can Meet the Japanese Challenge* (New York: Perseus, 1981). See also Richard T. Pascale and Anthony G. Athos, *The Art of Japanese Management: Applications for American Executives* (New York: Simon and Schuster, 1981).

8. David Halberstam, *The Best and the Brightest* (New York: Random House, 1969), 17.

9. "State of the Information Processing Industry," American Federation of Information Processing Societies, May, 1966.

10. U.S. Department of Education, *Digest of Education Statistics* (Washington, DC: Office of Vital Statistics, 2003), Table 56 (1962) and Table 256 (2001). Washington, DC: U.S. Government Printing Office.

11. See Jean Lipman-Blumen and Harold J. Leavitt, *Hot Groups: Seeding Them, Feeding Them, and Using Them to Ignite Your Organization* (New York: Oxford University Press, 1999). See also Warren Bennis and Patricia Ward Biederman, *Organizing Genius: The Secrets of Creative Collaboration* (New York: Perseus, 1997).

12. For more on skunk works, see Jay Miller, *Lockheed Martin's Skunk Works* (North Branch, MN: Specialty Press, 1996). See also Thomas J. Peters and Robert H. Waterman, *In Search of Excellence: Lessons from America's Best-Run Companies* (New York: Harper & Row, 1982), 211–212.

13. A fuller set of these notes was published earlier in Jean Lipman-Blumen and Harold J. Leavitt, *Hot Groups*.

14. Scott Thurm, "After the Boom, Cisco Is Learning to Go Slow," *Wall Street Journal*, 7 May 2003, 1.

Chapter 5

1. Ruth Leeds Love, "The Absorption of Protest," in *Readings in Managerial Psychology*, 4th ed., eds. Harold J. Leavitt, Louis R. Pondy, and David M. Boje (Chicago: University of Chicago Press, 1989), 471–497.

2. Ibid.

3. James C. Collins and Jerry I. Porras, *Built to Last: Successful Habits of Visionary Companies* (New York: HarperCollins, 1994), 95.

4. Hewlett Packard, "HP History and Facts," <http://www.hp.com/hpinfo/abouthp/histnfacts/> (accessed 25 May 2004).

5. "ABB's New Chief Promises Focus and a 'Sense of Urgency,'" *International Herald Tribune*, 24–25 November 2001.

6. Alvin Brown, *Organization of Industry* (New York: Prentice-Hall, 1947). The example is taken from p. 1 of a section titled "The Principles of Organization." Brown was a vice-president of Johns Manville Corp. and taught, on occasion, at MIT.

7. Harold J. Leavitt, "Technology: Where's the OFF Button?" *California Management Review* 44, 2 (Winter 2002), 126–140.

8. See, for example, Sheldon Krimsky, *Science in the Private Interest: Has the Lure of Profits Corrupted Biomedical Research?* (Lanham, MD: Rowman and Littlefield, 2003).

Chapter 6

1. *The Catholic Encyclopedia,* vol. VII (New York: Robert Appleton Company, 1910).

2. Douglas McGregor, "An Uneasy Look at Performance Appraisals," *Harvard Business Review* 35, 3 (1957), 89–94.

3. Ginka Toegal and Jay A. Conger, "360-degree Assessment: Time for Reinvention," *Learning and Education* 2, 3 (2003), 297–311.

4. T. W. Adorno et al., *The Authoritarian Personality* (New York: Harper, 1950).

5. Robert Levering and Milton Moskowitz, "100 Best Companies to Work For," *Fortune*, 20 January 2003, 127–152.

6. William F. Scandling, *The Saga of Saga: The Life and Death of an American Dream* (Mill Valley, CA: Vista Linda Press, 1994), xiii.

7. Carl F. Frost, John H. Wakely, and Robert A. Ruh, *The Scanlon Plan for Organization Development: Identity, Participation, and Equity* (East Lansing: Michigan State University Press, 1974).

8. *Social-instrumental* is a term coined by Jean Lipman-Blumen to describe one of nine achieving styles in *Connective Leadership: Managing in a Changing World* (New York: Oxford University Press, 2000).

9. Jean Lipman-Blumen and Harold J. Leavitt, *Hot Groups: Seeding Them, Feeding Them, and Using Them to Ignite Your Organization* (New York: Oxford University Press, 1999).

10. For a thorough analysis of power in organizations, its uses and misuses, see Jeffrey Pfeffer, *Managing with Power: Politics and Influence in Organizations* (Cambridge, MA: Harvard Business School Press, 1994).

11. Sophocles, *Antigone,* revised and updated by Paul Roche (London: Meridian, 1996), 205.

12. Susan Pulliam, "Ordered to Commit Fraud, a Staffer Balked, Then Caved," *Wall Street Journal,* 23 June 2003, 1.

Chapter 7

1. James MacGregor Burns, George R. Goethals, and Georgia J. Sorenson, eds., *Encyclopedia of Leadership* (Thousand Oaks, CA: Sage Publications, 2004).

2. Dave Barry, "I, Too, Have Worn a Military Flight Suit," *International Herald Tribune,* 31 May 2003, 20.

3. James MacGregor Burns, *Leadership* (New York: Harper and Row, 1978). Burns's seminal book discusses two kinds of leaders: transforming and transactional leaders. Burns's *transforming* leaders map pretty well to those whom others also call *leaders,* and his *transactional* leaders are closer to what many others call *managers.* See also Bernard M. Bass, *Transformational Leadership: Industrial, Military, and Educational Impact* (Mahwah, NJ: Lawrence Erlbaum Associates, 1998).

4. John W. Gardner, *On Leadership* (New York: Free Press, 1990), 1.

5. Jean Lipman-Blumen, *The Allure of the Toxic Leader: Why We Follow Destructive Bosses and Corrupt Politicians and How We Can Survive Them* (New York: Oxford University Press, 2005).

6. For a fine example, see Robert C. Cialdini, *Influence: The New Psychology of Modern Persuasion* (New York: Quill, 1984).

7. Deborah Solomon, "Inside Alleged Fraud at HealthSouth, a 'Family Plot,'" *Wall Street Journal,* 3 April 2003, 1 and A12.

8. See, for example, Edgar H. Schein, *Coercive Persuasion: A Socio-Psychological Analysis of the "Brainwashing" of American Civilian Prisoners by the Chinese Communists* (New York: W.W. Norton & Company, 1961).

9. Abraham Zaleznik, "Managers and Leaders: Are They Different?" *Harvard Business Review* (May–June 1977), 3 and 7. Quotes are from a version reprinted as an HBR Classic, *Harvard Business Review* (March–April 1992).

10. Warren Bennis, *On Becoming a Leader: The Leadership Classic—Updated and Expanded* (Cambridge, MA: Perseus, 2003), 39–40.

Chapter 8

1. The three-phase model is described more fully in Harold J. Leavitt, *Corporate Pathfinders* (New York: Penguin Books, 1987).

2. See, for example, three studies, decades apart: Sune Carlson, *Executive Behavior* (Stockholm: Strombergs, 1951); Henry Mintzberg, *The Nature of Managerial Work* (New York: Harper and Row, 1973); and John Kotter, "What Effective General Managers Really Do," *Harvard Business Review* (November–December 1982), 156–167.

3. See Robert B. Cialdini, *Influence: The New Psychology of Modern Persuasion* (New York: Quill, 1984).

4. A good resource is Daniel Goleman, *Emotional Intelligence: Why It Can Matter More Than IQ* (New York: Bantam, 1995).

5. W. E. B. Dubois, "The Conservation of Races," *The American Negro Academy Occasional Papers*, 2 (1897), Blackmask Online, <http://www.blackmask.com/books85c/conradex.htm> (accessed 25 May 2004).

Chapter 9

1. John W. Gardner, *On Leadership* (New York: Free Press, 1990), 98.

2. Jean Lipman-Blumen, *Connective Leadership: Managing in a Changing World* (New York: Oxford University Press, 2000), 1.

3. Harold J. Leavitt, "Beyond the Analytic Manager," Part I, *California Management Review* XVII, 3 (1975), 5–12, and Part II, XVII,4, 11–21.

4. For an excellent reminder, see Richard R. Ellsworth, *Leading with Purpose: The New Corporate Realities* (Stanford, CA: Stanford University Press, 2002).

INDEX

ABOUT THE AUTHOR

Harold J. Leavitt is Kilpatrick Professor of Organizational Behavior and Psychology, Emeritus at the Stanford University Graduate School of Business.

Professor Leavitt holds a bachelor's degree from Harvard University, an M.S. from Brown University, and a Ph.D. from the Massachusetts Institute of Technology. He served on the faculties of the University of Chicago and Carnegie Mellon University before coming to Stanford. He has also taught at the London Business School and at INSEAD in France.

Dr. Leavitt is the author of *Managerial Psychology,* now in its fifth edition and eighteenth language, *Corporate Pathfinders, Hot Groups* (with Jean Lipman-Blumen), and other books. His writings have appeared in the *Harvard Business Review,* the *Administrative Science Quarterly, Management Science,* and a number of other professional journals.

For several years, Professor Leavitt served as director of the Stanford Executive Program. He was also the first director of the Stanford-National University of Singapore Executive Program (SNUSEP), as well as an educational advisor to Thailand's Institute for Management Education. He has consulted with many organizations, including Bell Telephone Laboratories, the Ford Foundation, Kaiser Permanente, Varian Associates, and the Straits Times Press of Singapore. He is on the advisory boards of the University of Southern California's Leadership Institute, the Helsinki University of Technology's Euro-MBA Program, and the Institute for Advanced Studies in Leadership at Claremont Graduate University.

Dr. Leavitt's vocational interests include the functioning of small groups, communication networks, styles of thinking, management education, and the problems and pitfalls of accelerating technology. You may contact him via e-mail at: hjleavitt@earthlink.net.